An Arrow Returned

An Arrow Returned

CORRINE VANDERWERFF

REVIEW AND HERALD PUBLISHING ASSOCIATION
Washington, DC 20039-0555
Hagerstown, MD 21740

Copyright © 1986 by Review and Herald Publishing
Association

Edited by Raymond H. Woolsey
Book designed by Richard Steadham
Cover art by Bryan Leister

Printed in U.S.A.

Library of Congress Cataloging in Publication Data

Vanderwerff, Corrine.
    An arrow returned.

    1. Kongolo Kalumba wa Muhunga-Nday.   2. Converts,
Seventh-day Adventist—Zaire—Biography.   I. Title.
BX6189.K66Y36   1986   248.2'44'0924   [B]   86-17056

ISBN 0-8280-0364-5

Dedicated

with love to

Date

and Jon

and Joann and Richard

1

"Tutu! What's that?" The thrill of fear edged Kabange's (Kah-ban-gee) voice. He stopped, his small body rigid, blocking the trail in front of his companions.

"It's nothing!" Dominique replied quickly. Yet even as he spoke, his hand tightened on the wooden handle of his hunting knife, and his muscles tensed in readiness to draw it quickly from its sheath.

"But Tutu! Look! Loo . . ." Kabange's voice shivered away to almost nothing.

"Look! Tutu!" Kyungu (Kee-yoon-goo) echoed his twin brother sharply. "The tree!"

In the subdued sunlight that filtered through the overhead tangle of branches, vines, and leaves, he saw what stopped his younger brothers. Along with their cousin Mayombo (May-yohmboh), they froze into a tight triangle, not daring to move. Ahead on a low-hanging branch, a slender body looped tightly, its head raised and swaying ever so slightly as if daring them to take one step nearer.

"Mambala!" Even pronouncing its name made his mouth feel dry. "Don't move!" He held his knife in readiness, his mind working rapidly. He dared not close in on the snake with such a short knife, nor even with the machete that Kyungu carried. He glanced quickly around. There. Almost by his side. A knotted branch. He reached over and tested it with his free hand. Almost immediately the sharply honed blade of his knife was eating through it. Deftly slicing off the springy tips, he soon held in his hand a club slightly longer than his own body.

"Stay back!" he warned as he moved stealthily around the three frightened boys. In a semicrouch he neared the branch. Stopping short of the snake's reach, he drew back his weapon in the fashion of one who has learned a self-reliance beyond his years. Taking careful aim and drawing from every ounce of his body weight, he swung. He felt, more than saw, the club connect. As he recoiled for another blow, the snake seemed to lose its hold. Its coils relaxed and it slithered limply to the path, landing in a lazy sprawl.

"Tutu . . ."

"Stay back!" Dominique barked the command this time. Club still ready, he advanced. But the snake lay on a cushion of dead leaves, not moving. He dropped the club and unsheathed his knife again. Bending down, with a quick stroke he severed the triangular head from the dark body.

With victory yelps, the three younger boys rushed toward him.

"Be careful!" He stood quickly as if to bar their way.

Startled, the boys stopped.

"Mind where you are going. You don't want to step on that head and get poison in your foot!" He motioned them to the side of the path. "Here. We need to get this buried, so no one will walk on it."

With the machete they carved a hole in the ground. Using branches, they brushed the head and remains of the snake into the hole and buried them. Stamping the dirt into place, Dominique felt the responsibility of being "Tutu," the elder brother, lift momentarily, and he was again a little boy with his brothers.

"You killed the snake!" they chanted.

"I killed the snake!" he echoed.

Soon the words wound themselves into a song. Their small, bare feet pounded out the rhythm on the beaten path, their hands clapped the accompaniment. "Tu-tu! Am-ba! The snake! The snake!" They gave themselves to their dance of victory, their excited voices rising through the tangled, vine-draped trees. "Ha! Ha! Our enemy is dead!"

Suddenly Dominique stopped. "Come," he ordered sternly. "We cannot foolishly dance away our day. We have work to do." He picked up his knife and knotted the cord around his waist, positioning the sheath in readiness at his side. Kyungu picked up the machete and took the lead position. Kabange followed. Mayombo carried their pouch-shaped hunting bag woven from soft bamboo. Dominique, as always, was last. As Tutu he must walk behind the others, giving them the sense of his protection.

"This is going to be a lucky day!" exclaimed Mayombo. "Tutu has killed the wicked snake. And I am sure we will have many birds in our snares this afternoon."

"Fat ones too," added Kyungu. "Many of them. Enough for the papa and all the mamas and the uncle and the grandma . . ."

As the boys chattered on, Dominique was remembering his grandmother's words, the same words she spoke to them every afternoon when they left to check their traps. "Go well," she had said, touching the bamboo bag slung from Mayombo's shoulder. "May the great God accompany you and may you return with much food for us tonight."

It almost seemed to him that the ways of the village had always been his ways; that he had always gone with his brothers early in the morning beyond their mamas' fields to set their snares, and again in the afternoon to take their catch; that he had always known how to place the stakes and loop the slender cord and set the springy branch and arrange the bait of dried cassava leaves to tempt the birds.

Yet beyond all that, faint rememberings of the city stirred within him—of the White people his father used to work with, of the war and shooting they had fled, and of the independence the villagers spoke of so proudly.

"The colonists no longer rule our country." Dominique

remembered the happiness in the old grandfather's eyes. "It is our country now. We can decide our own future. We can plan our own progress." The stooped man, his long tattered cloth knotted around his waist, his floppy hat shading his face, had bent even closer, tapping a bony finger on Dominique's chest. "And that future, that progress, is for you, our children, for you."

Dominique could remember his father shaking his head sadly. "The ways of the village are not the ways of the city." He had spoken slowly. "We have our independence. We have returned to the village of our people. It is good that you grow up understanding the ways of our people—the two ways, the ways of the city and the ways of the village." He remembered the seriousness of his father's voice.

"But you must promise me these things," his father had continued. "You must promise me that you will never, never go anywhere alone with anyone you do not know. You must promise me that you will never, never eat the food of anyone you do not know. And you must promise me that you will never, never discuss those things that cannot be understood with anyone you do not know."

At first Dominique did not comprehend.

"There are powers, evil powers, powers many times stronger than even the strongest man, that can be used against those who do not keep their guard," his father had explained. "The light of the missions has not reached all the people of our villages. You must always be very careful. If you are, you will have nothing to fear. If not . . ."

Dominique accepted his father's warnings. The village soon became home, and the ways of the village, his ways. His people were hunters. He dreamed of the day he would be able to carry a strong bow with arrows that shoot swiftly and silently. He dreamed of the time he would have a gun, as his father had. He even dreamed of someday having a powerful rifle, such as belonged to those who had learned to hunt with the White man.

"I will hunt the antelope and the gazelle," he told himself. "And the prowling lion. And even the huge beast, the beast Papa has told about that has the size of a house and walks on legs that are round as trees. The one that has the force of many lions and the long nose with the strength to pull down the trees of the forest."

"But one cannot just kill any of God's creatures."

His mother's warnings wove through his thoughts.

"We must take only that which we can eat. And protect ourselves from that which is dangerous."

"As I killed the snake that was in our path today," Dominique told himself.

By now the boys had broken out of the forested area and were following the well-worn path that led toward the village fields and their own hunting grounds. Dominique's thoughts raced on. "Do you remember Kamina?" His father's question of the night before tangled itself with his idea of becoming a mighty hunter. "Do you remember the big houses? The good roads? The cars and the trucks? The nice clothes the people wore?"

Dominique vaguely remembered. But he preferred to think of new ways to prepare his snares so he could trap more birds.

"Don't you want to live in a nice house? To have nice clothes? To even have your own car someday?"

Something about his father's voice lodged the questions in his mind. "But don't we live in a good house?" he had asked, looking along the row of brown-red mud-brick houses with their roofs of gray thatch that stretched beside other rows of brown-red mud-brick houses with roofs of gray thatch that filled the village. "Doesn't our house keep us dry when the rains come? And don't we have good kitchen houses for my mama and the other mama?"

"Yes," his father had agreed. "Our house is as good as any house in the village. But don't you remember the houses in the city—the ones that have water that comes inside, and power, so that when it is night it can be light inside, and many rooms, enough for all the children? Wouldn't you like to have a house like that?"

Again his tone of voice had carried the words deep into Dominique's mind. It was as if his father was trying to tell him something about the past, something that was also important about the future. "Yes, Papa," he had responded. "I would like to have a house like that." He knew that this was the answer his father wanted. Still, he did not understand the total importance of the idea. "But I always want to be close to you and to Mama, and the little brothers and the sister, and to the other mama and her girl, who is our big sister."

His father had smiled. "That is not to say that we would not be near you. Tell me, though, how is it that these people in the city have their nice things? Does the government give them to them? Do their parents give them to them?" Without waiting for an answer, he continued. "No. They had to study, to learn, to go to school. . ."

There it was again. That word. School! He tried to avoid thinking of it. Yet in a few days, he too would be leaving for school. He remembered the day the village chief had called all the families together.

"We don't know where we are going in this world," the chief had begun. "Children, we are talking to you especially." The chief's words flowed through Dominique's thoughts. "School is for you. We, your parents, did not have the opportunity to study. In the old days, the colonists wanted the children to study. We preferred to hunt. Today you are our children. Tomorrow you will be in charge. Do you want to always keep things as they are? Do you want only to hunt?"

Within himself Dominique had wanted to say, "Yes. Yes, I want always to hunt." But he said nothing aloud.

"We won't always be with you," the chief had continued. "Be serious about school."

"School?" Dominique had asked himself. "It is a place to learn. That is true. It is good to know many things, to prepare for the future. It is good to know how to snare birds, to kill snakes. Someday we will be good hunters. We will provide food for the entire village. We will protect our people. But, school?"

The forest opened up into fields, and the four boys slowed their pace. They ducked to avoid brushing through clumps of the tall, heavy-bladed savanna grass that drooped down to tickle their shoulders. They skirted clumps of the shorter, coarse, white-veined grass. As they neared the place of their first snare, Dominique slipped ahead of the others. Silently he parted the grass that blocked his view, his body tensed to spring. Before him a plump field bird, one leg secured by the cord of the snare, pecked absentmindedly at the dry shreds of cassava still on the ground.

Hurtling himself forward, Dominique grasped the bird with two hands, letting his left hand slide quickly back to pinion the wings. With the other hand he slipped his knife out. Immediately Mayombo was at his side, the bamboo game bag ready to receive their first catch of the day. Kyungu and Kabange deftly unstrung the snare, looped up the cord, and gathered the slender pegs.

Dominique dropped the bird into the bag, a smile stretching broadly across his dark face, his brown eyes snapping with anticipation. "A good omen!" he exclaimed. "You are right. We will have many birds today. The grandmother will be happy." He paused a moment. Suddenly he placed himself in front of the other three. "Someday," he spoke firmly, gravely. "Someday we will be great hunters. We will bring home much meat for our families and for our village. When we're big. When we have guns like Papa. Will you respect me then as you do now? Will you always honor my words as your older brother? Will you always call me Tutu?"

Three sets of deep-brown eyes stared up at him. Three moon-round faces regarded him solemnly. Three little heads nodded with sincerity. "Always, Tutu." It was Kyungu who spoke. As the firstborn of the twins—even his name meant "he who comes first"—he was the one to respond for the others.

"Always?" Dominique demanded.

"Always," responded Kyungu.

"Even when we are very big?"

"Even when we are very big."

"Even when I go away to school—and when I come back—will I still be Tutu? Will I still be your leader when we go hunting?"

"When you hunt. Even when you go away to school. We will always be the ones to carry for you."

"Promise?"

"Promise."

"Papa has said that I must go away next week. You know that, don't you?"

Silence.

"You know that I must go away next week, don't you? That Papa has said that I must go to school?" Dominique spoke even more loudly.

The three heads nodded again. Still, none of them spoke. It seemed that tears wanted to roll out of Kabange's eyes. "But, Tutu," he managed at last. "Tutu, we don't want you to go away."

"When you go, who will take us hunting?" broke in Mayombo. "Who will be here to protect us?"

Nearly half a head taller than the others, Dominique regarded them thoughtfully. "We have hunted together since you have been big enough to walk beyond the sight of the mama's eyes. You know how to set the snares. You have watched me as I bagged the birds we have caught. You know all the paths. You know how to use your eyes to watch for danger. Were you not the one who first saw the snake this afternoon, Kabange? You are now as big as the other boys in the village when they began to make their own traps. When I am gone, Kyungu will be the one who walks behind to see that no danger can harm you."

He stopped speaking, as if the matter were settled, and half turned. "Come, now," he said. "We cannot stand here and talk all day. We must hurry to our other traps before the shadows become too long. We must not cause our mamas any worry. Besides, it is another week before I go to school."

That night, as they had hoped, their catch was enough for the entire family. Their grandmother and all the mamas congratulated them loudly. After eating, Dominique stretched out on a mat beside the fire, his stomach full and content. The twins and Mayombo had told and retold the story of the snake, and he still basked in the praise of all the parents. Even so, his thoughts continued to stray.

"The snake," he mused. Lying by the fire, half drowsy, the voices of the adults comfortably close, he felt no fear, no anxiety. In the forest, they feared nothing more than the deadly serpent, which could strike without warning. Now in the courtyard by the evening fire, danger seemed far away. Then other words came unbidden to mind. "The serpent wants to curse me."

2
Despite the coziness Dominique felt, a shiver contorted his spine. He reached out with a piece of branch and poked at the glowing coals. A shower of sparks sprayed up, then disappeared into the night. "Dangers," he mused. "Dangers that can't be seen." His father's warnings echoed through his thoughts. "Evil powers. Powers many times more evil than snakes."

He poked at the coals again. "Never, never eat with strangers. Not lemons, not oranges, not pineapples—not anything. If you want something, get it yourself. Or ask me. Even here. In our own village. You must always be careful." He watched the tiny sparks drift upward and fade into nothingness.

"Just a little time before we came, one of the papas in this very village lost a son he loved very much—a schoolboy like you are going to be." Dominique knew he would never ever forget the story his father told. "One day as he was out walking by himself, a man called to him. 'Come with me,' he invited. 'I know where to find some very good pineapples in the forest. Come and we can eat together.'

"Hungry, the boy gladly followed the friendly stranger. They walked deeper and deeper into the forest. At last the man stopped and sat on a fallen log. He gestured for the boy to sit also. The boy looked around. He saw no pineapples. The man smiled a strange smile—then made a quick gesture with his hand. Instantly, plates and knives and forks appeared on the log between them. Out of nowhere pineapples materialized on the plates. Horrified, the boy stared at the plates of pineapple.

"The man laughed a little, then picked up his knife and fork to begin eating. 'You have seen,' he said quickly. 'Now you are one of us. You must eat.'

"With deepening horror, the boy realized what had happened. Our ancestors have taught us that when a man is tricked into seeing secret things of the spirit world, he becomes impure and can never escape the spell. At that moment the person becomes a sorcerer and will remain one for the rest of his life. Believing that, the boy took up his knife and fork and began to eat.

"The man continued to talk as they ate. 'Our magic exists to trap people,' he explained. 'Someone of your family is demanded. If it is not to be you, then you must cast a spell on one of the others—your mother, a sister, a brother . . .'

"The boy walked home, changed but not changed. Outwardly he still looked the same. Inwardly he carried a heavy, dark secret, a secret he knew he could never escape. At home he talked with his father as if nothing had happened. While he was talking he began to stare at a spot on the ground ahead of him. 'Papa!' he suddenly shrieked. 'The serpent wants to curse me!' With that, his mouth clamped shut. He tried to say something more, but each time he opened his mouth to speak, it would mysteriously clamp shut.

"Suspecting what might have happened, the family counseled together. 'We must make an *effort* to save our boy,' they agreed. 'To make an effort' meant that they would search for a fetisher [witch doctor], who would tell them the boy's problem and suggest a cure.

"After receiving payment of a chicken, the fetisher consulted his magic potions. 'A spell has been cast on your son,' he told the father at last, naming the sorcerer responsible. 'Someone in your family is to die. Be careful. It may be you.'

"In the manner of those with faith in the fetishers, the father went to find the sorcerer. 'Why does my boy not talk anymore?' he demanded.

" 'I will come to discuss the matter,' the sorcerer agreed.

"He came. The family gathered around in a group with the sorcerer and they talked, for that is the manner in which such sorcerers 'cure' their victims. The sorcerer then spoke a strange word, took the boy's hand, and spat into it. 'Your boy will have his voice back,' he said. 'He will again speak as normal. But the price is that he will be a sorcerer for the rest of his life.'

"By evening the boy did have his voice back. He spoke as he always had. Not long after, however, he fell ill. Day by day he became weaker. His father sat by his bed. 'Papa.' The boy's eyes were dull with fever, yet he spoke with intensity. 'Papa. This world is full of evil things. I have seen the world that is impure. Remember the day I lost my voice? Remember how I told you the serpent wanted to curse me? I saw that serpent on the ground. I was tricked into the forest that morning by the sorcerer. I saw strange things done in the spirit world.'

"The boy told what had happened in the forest. 'But one cannot announce the secrets of that world and be safe,' he continued. 'If I die, it is because of sorcery. If I do not die, then I must cast a spell on someone else in our family. I do not want anyone innocent to die. Papa, you must warn the others. You must warn them of the world of the impure spirits.'

"The boy died that night. When the people came to mourn with the family, the father told them the boy's story. And now you know why I warn you to be careful. Here in Africa such traps of the evil one are many. The Bible warns us against these powers of darkness. That is why God has given us His angels. Always put your faith in God. Always ask for the protection of His angels."

Dominique raised himself and stared into the dying fire. "Why do people always go to the fetishers to search for protection?" he asked himself. "Why don't they ask God for His angels?" He continued to stare thoughtfully at the fire. I wonder? He thought ahead to the next week. I wonder, does school teach us about God? Will it teach us how to always be safe from the evil one?

3 "A-e-i-o-u. A-e-i-o-u." The sounds of the vowels filled every corner of the room. Row after row of their scrawled shapes marched across slates, then faded with a smudge of a hand, only to have to be made again.

"And again," the teacher ordered.

"A-e-i-o-u. A-e-i-o-u." Dominique mouthed the sounds automatically. He was squeezed into a classroom with 70 other beginners. They sat two and even three students each at heavy wooden desks in a Catholic mission school. Dominique began to wonder if school would ever be anything more than repeating letters and tracing their shapes on his slate. The monotonous tread of the rhythm made him want to put his head down and cover his ears with his hands. His entire body felt tired.

"A-e-i-o-u." Every day when they entered school, they had to leave Kiluba, the language they had always spoken, at the door. Every day they stepped into a world of only Swahili and French. "A-e-i-o-u. A . . . " Dominique felt his head growing heavier and his thoughts straying. "A . . . an antelope. A big one. I've never before seen such a big one. The grandfather . . . " His head continued to sag, but his thoughts sprang alive.

"It's very dangerous to walk here." His grandfather's warnings of the day before had held him back from the temptation to race ahead. As they went deeper and deeper into the forest, Dominique took in every word his grandfather said. "No one, not even the wisest person, would suspect our traps. That is why the chiefs forbid everyone else to come here." Carrying his grandfather's machete, Dominique had felt very important.

"We dig a deep hole in the path," his grandfather continued. "Wide at the top, narrow below. Covered with branches, sodded, and strewn with leaves, no one would suspect . . . Whatever falls in will be wedged firmly at the bottom."

Suddenly, a few steps ahead, the path seemed to have caved away. They approached cautiously. "E-o!" Dominique exclaimed, looking over the edge. "It's big."

"God has been good." His grandfather's gaze followed his. "There will be food for many families." He looked at Dominique thoughtfully. "Quickly. Run to your uncle. Tell him we need many men to lift this antelope. And many mamas to carry the meat."

Dominique forced himself to run his fastest.

"Dominique!"

Dominique pulled his thoughts back to the present.

"Dominique. Is something wrong?"

"No, Teacher." He shook his head and again bent over his slate.

"You seem very tired today."

Dominique shook his had again. He did not want to tell how they had found the big antelope in the pit trap, how he had raced back to the village, how he wished he could always go hunting with his grandfather. He forced his attention back to his slate.

"Dominique!"

It was Bukama, his friend from his home village, running to catch up with him after class.

"Dominique, aren't you tired of all this school every day?"

Dominique nodded.

"We need to quit." Bukama blurted the words out quickly. "We need to quit school."

"Quit school?" Surprise underlined Dominique's voice.

Bukama nodded.

"But our papas brought us to live here so we could study. What would they say?"

"We would explain," Bukama replied. "What is the sense of school anyway? What is the good of all this a-e-i-o-u? What is the use of learning Swahili and French?"

"The chief and our papas have said it is important."

"Ha!" exclaimed Bukama. "Do they have to sit inside on hard benches all day?"

"They have said it is good for our future."

"What can school do for our future?"

"We study."

"Mmmmph!" snorted Bukama. "Can we eat Swahili? Can we eat French?"

In spite of himself, Dominique smiled.

"Just think about our little brothers, what they are learning while we are locked up at those miserable desks." Bukama pressed his argument. "They are out setting the traps we should be setting. They are catching the animals we should be catching. They are learning how to feed our families. And when we are big, what will we know? A-E-I-O-U!"

As Bukama poured out his disgust, Dominique felt his own distaste for school growing. He knew that back home at that very moment the little brothers would be watching by the house. They would be waiting for the shadow to reach the line they had scratched deeply into the beaten earth of the courtyard, so that they would know it was the time of the afternoon—not too early and not too late—to go to the snares they had set in the morning. Thinking of them and looking at Bukama standing defiantly in front of him, he longed for the forest and the fields.

"We could go home." Bukama spoke matter-of-factly now. "We could tell our papas that we have tried school. We could tell them that we have found that it is not good."

With all of his heart Dominique wanted to say, "Yes. Let's go. Let's tell our papas that school is not good." But something stopped him. He shook his head slowly. "I promised Papa that I would be serious about school," he replied. "I promised him that, now matter how difficult it was or how lonely I felt, I would study."

"But you can see that school is no good for our future. Think about our traps. With only the little time on weekends, what can we learn about hunting?"

"I know." Dominique spoke resignedly. "But I promised Papa. And if I promised Papa . . . "

"But if you explained to him . . . "

Dominique sighed. Suddenly he brightened with a new idea. "I'll tell you what," he offered. "I can't quit now. But when the holidays come, and we can go home—we will talk to our papas then. We will tell them how we have spent a whole year at school. We will tell them that it has not helped us at all. We will tell them that the forest is the real school that will prepare us for the future. We will tell them that knowing Swahili and French will never help us feed our families."

The school year finally dragged to a close. When he received his report card, Dominique was surprised to find that he was among the top in his class. The important and exciting thing, though, was that he could go home.

"And we'll talk to our papas just as soon as we get there?" Bukama reminded him when they left the classroom on the last day.

Dominique nodded.

The days at home sped into a blur of happiness. His father was so pleased with the report card that he could hardly speak of anything else.

"When are we going to talk to our papas?" Bukama kept asking.

"Later," Dominique would reply. "My papa is not yet in the frame of mind to accept that idea."

"But I'll help you explain."

"We'd better wait a little while."

"I'm tired of your little whiles. Let's do it tomorrow."

"Oh, OK," Dominique agreed reluctantly. "But I don't think it's the time yet."

As he was falling asleep that night, Dominique sorted through ideas of how best to convince his father.

"Oo-hee-oohee-oohee-oo-heo-hee . . . "

The hollow, haunting call cut through any further idea of sleep. Dominique jumped from his bed. Kyungu and Kabange stirred.

"What is it, Tutu?" Kyungu asked sleepily.

"The call to a big hunt." Dominique already had his old hunting shorts on and was pulling on his shirt. "I'm going to see."

He pushed out of the house into the predawn. Above the savanna that stretched to the east of the village, a faint golden haze was starting to fill the sky. He ran lightly along the hardened path that led between the family compounds.

"My son. Where are you going so quickly, so soon in the day?"

Surprised by his father's voice, Dominique halted abruptly. "The hunt?" he asked quickly. "Is there a hunt?"

His father smiled at his eagerness. "Yes. I'm just going for my gun."

"And I can come?"

His father shook his head. "Not today. Only hunters with the strongest weapons are allowed. It will be very dangerous."

"Dangerous?"

"Elephants."

Dominique's eyes grew big. "Elephants!" he repeated excitedly. Visions of the enormous beasts his father had earlier tried to explain to him galloped through his thoughts. "I want to see them!"

His father laid a restraining hand on his shoulder. "They passed by in the night, headed west. The big hunter who has been visiting the chief will lead the hunt. When it is safe, we will send for you."

"But, Papa . . . "

"No. This is no hunt for children."

Dominique watched as his father hurried off to join the others. With all his heart he wanted to race after him. But he just stood there watching, until the men, most carrying guns but some carrying heavy spears, disappeared from view. Suddenly Dominique sprang to life.

"Bukama!" he yelled, racing off in the direction of his friend's house. "Bukama! Let's follow the hunters!"

Bukama stared at him strangely. "Do we dare?"

"We'll take weapons."

"What will the hunters say?"

"They're far ahead. We can prepare now, then leave when the sun reaches the top of the sky. That way we should meet the messenger on his way to get us. We will miss the hunt, but we will be the first from the village . . . "

Bukama's dark eyes sparkled with excitement as he began to understand his friend's plan. "I'll get my bow and arrows!" he exclaimed. "Elephants! Wheeee! Let's go!"

The boys raced off to prepare for their journey.

4 Letting out a shrill whoop, Dominique burst from behind the last tree that had screened him from view and dashed into the circle of hunters. He held his bow and arrows triumphantly overhead. Suddenly he stopped short. All the haste and bravado that had pushed him to be first at the hunting site drained from his body. He dropped the bow to his side and let it rest on the ground.

"See our work." One of the men pointed toward what at first appeared to be a pile of brush.

Dominique stared in the direction he pointed.

"Big, isn't it?" the man asked.

Dominique continued to stare. The men stood in little clusters about the branch-covered mound. Trees were strewn haphazardly here and there as if someone had hurriedly slashed the clearing with a monster machine. He forced his eyes away from the mound to look at the men. "Papa!" he shouted, spotting his father. He ducked his head and dashed toward him. "Papa, is ..." He pressed close to his father's side. "Is it really dead?"

His father cupped his hand about Dominique's shoulder and gave it a comforting squeeze. "Yes, my son, it is really dead."

Dominique found himself staring again. "It's big!" His voice was nothing more than a whisper.

Some of the men started to pull back the branches from the gigantic body. As they did so, Dominique drew back behind his father as if afraid the elephant might suddenly rise to its feet and rush toward him. "Did—did you kill it with those branches?" he asked. "Is that why there are so many?"

Chuckling, his father reached back and pulled him again to his side. "Think," he said. "Think, my boy. Could we fight a big animal like that with those little branches?"

Dominique stared at the animal and at the branches. Then he looked down at his own bow, which had suddenly seemed so useless when he had first seen the animal. "No, Papa," he said at last. "But why all those branches?"

"It's the habit of these animals," his father explained. "I will tell you about it. When we neared the elephants this morning, just over there where you see that the trees are thinner, the hunter signaled us back. He climbed a tree, then signaled us all to climb trees. He climbed down and crept silently to another tree even closer. From my tree I could see him and I could see the animals. He aimed his powerful rifle. When he shot, the biggest one started to circle dizzily. Suddenly there was a heavy noise, as of an approaching rain, as the other elephants raced into the forest, crashing through the underbrush, grabbing at trees and tearing them from their roots, all in a frenzied attempt to protect themselves.

"We were downwind—every one of us crouched, hidden, in a big tree, watching. Those gigantic animals raged about the forest. The big bull continued to stumble about, trying to follow them, moving his huge head from side to side as if to shake away that terrible thing that had exploded into his brain. Suddenly, with a terrible roar, he collapsed.

"Their leader down, the others stopped their dash. They returned and grouped themselves about him, prodding and pushing, trying to get him back on his feet. When he did not respond, they began to tear up small trees and to rip off leafy branches. They covered him with those. Then they marched quietly into the forest and were gone. Finally, the hunter said it was safe to come down."

Dominique continued to stare at the still mountain of an animal before him. Never had he seen anything so huge. Hesitatingly, he took a step toward it.

"Go ahead, my son. Touch it. Examine it."

Dominique made a big circle around it, then tentatively touched the side of a huge leg. Satisfied that the beast could no longer do him any harm, he grappled the leg in an attempt to climb. Then, fearful of falling, he slid back to the ground and went around to stare at the long nose.

"The elephant's strength," he heard someone say. "With his nose he can pick grass to eat. With it he can tear out trees as if they were small garden plants."

Dominique looked up at the one who was speaking. "Friend hunter," he exclaimed, "Thank you! Thank you!" And he clasped his hands together in the manner of one showing deep appreciation. "You have done well."

"And you?" asked the man. "Will you one day become a hunter like me? I can see how you are interested."

"But how?" Dominique asked. "How could I ever become a hunter like you?"

"The most important thing is that you must love to hunt," replied the man. "You must be courageous against such big animals. And you must be a man of decision."

"What age did you begin to learn this?"

"Me? I was almost grown when I began. Now I have had much experience. You, being very young, can grow up to do even greater things than I have done."

As the hunter spoke, Dominique felt an excitement growing. He wondered if this might not be the exact idea he needed to convince his father to allow him to quit school. At that moment he saw his father coming toward them. "Papa!" he exclaimed. "Isn't it wonderful what the hunter has done?"

"It takes a brave man with much experience to have killed such a dangerous beast," replied his father.

"Papa," Dominique began again. "He says I can learn to be a hunter someday—just like he is."

His father looked questioningly at the hunter. "Yes," the hunter said to Dominique. "Hunting is another study. It is necessary to learn many things in life. You need to learn things as you have the opportunity. I had the opportunity to learn from the big-game hunters. Here in the village you learn the ancestral ways—things you would never know in the city. But," and he looked straight at Dominique, "is it good to go to only one market?"

"Pardon?" asked Dominique, not sure of the question.

"Is it good to go to only one market?" repeated the man. "I mean, is it good to know only one way of life? If a person has lived only in the city, he does not understand the ways of the village. In order to understand them, it is necessary to go to the village and to live there.

"To become a good hunter," he continued, "is not easy. It is like being in the military. Along with courage, it takes drill and it takes discipline." He looked at Dominique's father. "To become a good hunter," he added, "is like following studies at school. Many things that one must learn are like the a-e-i-o-u. They seem unimportant. They take time. But if one is to have success, they must be mastered." He laid his hand on Dominique's shoulder. "I can see that you have the courage. Our people need good hunters. But our country is facing a new time. Always remember, the wise person goes to more than one market. Our people need men who have the courage to be wise in many ways."

A distant sound of many voices chanting neared quickly, growing into one loud voice that drowned further possibility of talk. The villagers swarmed into the clearing—older men beating drums and blowing horns; the women, with baskets on their heads, shrilling out their cries of happiness, cries formed with their tongues, much like the war whoop but with more rounded tones carrying a lilt of joy. Everyone flowed into the clearing, moving around the elephant until they formed a circle. Feet moved rhythmically with the continuous beat of the drums, while the cries and chants wove themselves into a song. Dominique found himself swept along with his father into the dance of victory. The hunter was pushed inside the circle, beside the elephant. Suddenly, as if by signal, the dancing and the singing stopped. The hunter drew himself up to his full height.

"Thank you. Thank you. Thank you for this recognition you have given me," he began. "Thank you for this appreciation for the skill that I learned from the White man when the colonists were still with us. Thank you for the bravery of your hunters who came with me."

Dominique wondered at the power, the deepness, of his voice.

The hunter talked of the art of hunting elephants and of the courage and daring involved. "Among you," he continued, "are children who one day can become hunters just as I am. When you came, I was just explaining to one of your children how hunting elephants demands a love, a courage, and a lack of fear in order to have success. A good hunter needs to be like a soldier."

Dominique listened proudly as the man repeated the words he had already told him.

"And you children, you who dream of becoming great hunters, don't let those dreams crowd out the attention you should give to your studies at school. As much as our people depend now on the courage of our hunters to provide food, our future and the future of our new country depends on you youngsters who have the courage and the discipline of soldiers. You need to have the courage to continue."

"The courage to continue." The words seemed to repeat themselves inside Dominique's head. "Courage to continue at school!" His hopes of having found the perfect argument to convince his father totally dashed, he found his mind starting to fill with new thoughts.

"The elephant is here." The hunter's words caught him back to the present. "For you. You may begin your work."

"Are we going to talk to our papas today?" Bukama asked on their way back to the village.

"After what the hunter said?"

"But you promised. And you know what he said about our people needing good hunters."

"And you heard what he said about school."

"You promised."

"We will talk to our fathers."

"Now?"

Dominique nodded.

Dominique's father was nearest. They hurried to catch up with him. "What?" he exploded when the boys made their proposition. "Quit school? You!" he exclaimed, turning on Bukama. "You can waste your life on your traps if you want—if your father is foolish enough to allow you to do that! And you!" He turned toward Dominique. "After what the hunter has said. You dare to think of such ideas!"

Dominique hung his head.

"After the report card you brought home! I thought that surely, surely you understood the importance of school. And now . . ."

Suddenly the words that Dominique was searching for were there. He felt a new confidence surge through his body. He lifted his head and faced his father squarely. He had kept his promise to Bukama. And he would go with him to his father, too. But first he must explain something.

"Papa." He spoke with determination. "Papa. I see the importance of knowing many things. I see the importance of knowing the ways of the village. I see the importance of knowing the ways of school. I see the importance of preparing for my future and for the future of my people. School is not easy. But, Papa, I have the courage to continue."

5

"Aha! The little colonist!"

Dominique felt his stomach tightening and his blood pumping faster.

"Colonist!"

Dominique straightened abruptly. "Don't you call me that!" he retorted.

"Colonist! Colonist!"

"Am not!" he shouted back. He dropped his mallet, fists ready to defend his words. "I'm as black as you are. And Luba!"

"Then why do you work? Why do you wear your pretty shoes? And your fancy clothes?"

"Because I want to," he shot back. "And if I want to have nice things, I have to work." He turned from his taunters and grabbed up his mallet. In his fury, he hit the peg too hard. Instead of pushing through the bamboo as it should, it twisted sideways, snapping off and splitting the piece it was supposed to anchor in place. Even more disgruntled, Dominique bent to pull off the length of bamboo he had been trying to fit into place.

"What's the matter, colonist?"

Dominique glowered up at the two boys. Their extra years of growth gave them more advantage than he cared to tackle. "Why don't you just go away?" He clucked his tongue in disdain.

"Problems?"

Dominique looked up with relief as his father came out of the main house.

"Naw. We're just leaving." The two boys turned and headed for the road that bordered the family compound.

"Why do they always have to say that?" Dominique demanded. "What's wrong with working the way I do?"

"There's absolutely nothing wrong with your working," his father replied. "But what do they say?"

"They always call me the colonist!" As he said the last word, he chomped his teeth down hard and clenched them. In his hurt, he felt the tears stinging in his eyes and he did not want to cry like a baby in front of his father.

"The colonist, you say," his father repeated. He reached down and tested the stack of bamboo just inside of the work shelter. "You don't like them to call you the colonist?"

Dominique shook his head emphatically and forced himself to speak. "The colonists are gone from our country. They no longer rule over us. We're free. We have our independence. I am not a colonist!"

His father sat down on the stack of bamboo. "Then why do they call you that?"

With his father's calm manner of asking questions, Dominique felt himself relaxing. "Because the little brothers and I wear shoes. And we have new shirts. And we wear socks. And we sometimes carry candies to eat at school during recreation."

"I see," replied his father. "And because of that they call you the colonist. So if you do not want to be called the colonist, you must stop doing those things?" He looked questioningly at Dominique.

A smile almost traced itself across Dominique's face. He nodded. "But we work for those things, the little brothers and I. We work for every sous [penny] we have."

His father nodded. "And the people know. But many refuse to understand. When you are caught in a time of change and you do not want to change, life can become very complicated. When the colonists were in our country, the people liked the things they brought. All the people want things. But they are not all willing to work. When someone else works and he is able to buy things, they become jealous.

"When the colonists were here, some took advantage of the people. They made them work hard and then barely paid them anything. Others taught us how to work and how to earn. Now we have our independence. We are free to find our own way. You have found a way to earn the money to buy things for yourself and for your little brothers. How many other boys have done that? How did you get the idea?"

Dominique shook his head. "I don't know, Papa. You have taught me to enjoy my studies, to be serious about preparing for my future. But the autos . . . I don't know, Papa. It is as I have told you before. It must be the great God who put the idea in my head. I have seen autos on the road that the rich people from the city have. I saw how people can make things from bamboo. And one day the idea just came for making these big cars that children can ride on."

"And do people like your cars?"

"We have orders for more than we can make."

"And do people tell you to stop making the cars?"

"No. They always ask for more."

"But they still call you the colonist."

Dominique nodded.

"Is it all bad to be called that?"

"I don't like it. It's . . . It's . . ."

"It's a word that puts a bad taste in your mouth," his father finished for him. "But the colonists are the ones who showed us how to live like this . . . Now that we have independence, we must choose. We can follow what the White man has shown us, or we can return to the ways of our ancestors. It seems that most people like the White man's clothes and his cars and his cookies and his candies. But not everyone likes his way of working. Yet work is necessary in order to have those things.

"No matter what you do, my son, you will have to choose

within yourself. You have chosen to make your autos. You buy shoes and clothes and school things. I am proud of you. And your mother is proud of you. Remember the counsel of the big hunter: 'The man who is wise goes to more than one market.' You have grown up with the ways of our people, of the hunters, of the village. Now we have come to this bigger village where we have our own school. You are a child of the future. Already you are developing understanding. One day you will have the responsibility of helping the people of our tribe, the Lubas, and the other peoples of our country. You will have to help them understand these new ways that must come if we are to have the progress we dreamed of when we got our independence."

Dominique nodded.

"Son, you don't have to be afraid of being 'the colonist.' As you say, the great God has shown you a way, and you have chosen it. Someday you will find a way to help others to understand."

"But Papa, how?"

"When the time is right, you will know."

Dominique pondered his father's words after he had left. He continued working on the car he had promised for the neighbor's little boy. Just as he and the three younger boys had hunted together, they now worked together building ride-on bamboo cars. "Uncle Sondashi was not an easy one to convince, though," he reminded himself. He remembered one afternoon the first year they had moved to Kitenge. It was near the end of his third year in school. The car idea was still new—they had built only a few. He remembered that afternoon as if it had been only the day before.

"Tutu! Tutu!"

It had been Mayombo.

"What is it?" he had demanded, noting Mayombo's anxiety.

"Tutu. My papa says we cannot build any more cars!"

"But why?"

"Because . . . oh, Tutu. He has taken our almost-finished one and thrown it into the big ditch." Mayombo's big eyes were already filling with tears.

"He's what?"

"Over there. And he said if we take it out . . ." Mayombo's chin trembled. "If we take it out, he's going to beat us."

Shocked, Dominique did not know what to do. An uncle has the same authority as a papa. One could not argue with him about his decision. His papa was away. "Just wait here," he told Mayombo. "Mama!" he called, running out to the kitchen house. "Uncle Sondashi has thrown our car into the ditch!"

"He's what?" His mother straightened up from the big pot of cassava dough she was stirring.

"Mayombo said Uncle Sondashi has thrown our car into the ditch and that he will beat us if we try to get it back."

"He can't do that!" exclaimed his mother. "Just you wait. We will see what he thinks he can do."

When his mother spoke like that, Dominique knew things would happen. When something touched her children, she was not afraid of speaking directly to man or beast. "I'll see what this brother has in his head," she continued. She gathered the gray-white mass of cassava dough into a big ball with her heavy wooden stirring spoon. Putting the lid on the pot, she pulled it to one side, balancing it on one cooking rock and the ground. She cut straight across the courtyard toward their uncle's house on the other side of the compound.

Dominique followed at a distance. Motioning the three younger boys to come, he pressed against the side of the house, in the shadow of the overhang, where they could watch and listen.

"What is this?" his mother demanded, marching straight to where the uncle was sitting outside of his house. "What have you done with the auto the boys were making?"

His uncle stood to face his mother. "Those boys are wasting too much time on that foolishness!" he exploded.

"Foolishness?" His mother's voice rose higher. "Foolishness? When they earn money! And buy shoes and shirts and—"

"Wasting their time and becoming tired when they should be concentrating all their energy at school!"

"And they are not doing well at school?" she demanded. "Are you saying these boys are not doing well at school? Who do you think was second in his class this term? Who?"

It seemed as if Uncle Sondashi had taken a step backwards.

"I'll tell you who," his mother fairly screamed. "Dominique was! And the twins? And your Mayombo? Tell me that none of them are leaders in their class!"

"But . . . But . . ."

"But nothing," his mother fumed. "Why do you have to stop what is good?"

Dominique and the others pressed tighter against the side of the house, listening.

"Don't take on so, sister," Uncle Sondashi finally said. "I will discuss this with my elder brother when he returns."

Reassured, the four boys slipped away and headed for the school yard to join in a game of soccer with their friends. Before many days, they were back at work on the cars—after promising that the work would never interfere with their studies.

"And it hasn't." Dominique carefully fitted another bamboo section into place then pegged it in firmly. "Uncle Sondashi is proud of our work now. The people like to buy our cars. But . . ." Dominique sighed.

"Someday you'll find a way to help the others to understand." His father's words echoed in his mind.

6 The sun dipped near the horizon, stretching the palm shadows into long, shaggy-topped blotches on the dusty road. The four boys, silent under heavy loads of peeled bamboo balanced on their shoulders, turned from the road into the path that led between the Protestant pastor's house and the school. Suddenly a throaty bark sounded behind them.

"Simba! Simba!" The pastor yelled.

The dog ignored his call and rushed on after the boys, a snarl accenting its barks.

Twisting around, Dominique felt his heart catch at the sight of the charging furry form. Gathering his strength, he hurled his heavy bundle into the dog's path. Three more heavy thuds sounded as the younger boys hurled their bamboo too.

"Run!" Dominique hollered, giving Kabange and Mayombo a

shove in the general direction of home. Kyungu already raced ahead. Dominique darted toward the dog, then swerved in the opposite direction from his brothers and cousin. As he hoped, the dog veered after him. Dominique's legs pumped in quick strides. His feet carried him forward, faster and faster. "Run!" his brain urged. "Run!"

Fear drove him on. He felt the dog closing in. Its snarl sent shivers down his back. He lengthened his stride, desperate to escape. Just then his right foot came down hard on a broken bit of brick. The jagged triangle crunched under the sudden weight, throwing him off balance. He felt himself pitching forward. He tried to gather his body into a tight roll, but his momentum sent him thudding heavily onto the hard earth and he spread into a contorted sprawl. In that moment he felt the dog tearing at his khaki shorts. He writhed, trying to escape. "Ma-ma-ma-ma-ma-ma . . ." Fear pitched his wails high.

"Simba! Stop!" Heavy footsteps rushed toward them. "Simba!" He felt the dog being pulled away. "Shame! To the house!" The voice shouted orders at the dog then calmed. "Boy?" Dominique felt someone touch his back gently. "Boy? Are you all right?"

Dominique raised his head slightly, hardly daring to look up. "Is he gone?"

"Yes. It's all right. Here. Let me help you."

A strong arm reached toward him, and Dominique felt himself being pulled to his feet. He stood shakily. Pulsing with fear, he felt paralyzed but noticed no pain.

"This is not good. Come. I will help you to my house. We will put some medicine . . ."

"Medicine." Startled by the word, Dominique reached to his back. A gaping rip stretched from the waist of his shorts. Something warm and stickly oozed out. He pulled his hand quickly away.

"Oh, I am so sorry. So sorry. We must clean that wound." The words rushed out. "Me! A pastor! My dog! Can you forgive me?"

Still stunned, Dominique found himself being gathered up into the pastor's arms. "Foolish dog," the pastor continued. "He's never hurt anyone before. He's always so playful. I never thought . . ." By this time a crowd of children had collected. They stood around the house while the pastor took Dominique in.

Finally he came back out holdng to his hip a clean handkerchief of the pastor's.

"We'll walk home with you," some of the older ones offered.

"Does it hurt?" a girl asked. Dominique shook his head.

"You know that when you are bitten by a dog, you will become very sick," a boy volunteered.

"Yes," offered another. "Very sick. You'll become sick in the head."

"You'll be crazy."

"That's true," agreed another. "Crazy in the head."

"And they will have to tie you up."

"With strong cords."

"You need very strong medicine. Many fetishes."

"Only the sorcerer can help."

"You can die."

The children's excited conversation swirled into a blur. "Crazy!" his head screamed at him. "The dog bit you. You'll be crazy." A new fear seized him. "Crazy!" He began to feel all wobbly and shaky again. Two of his friends put their arms around his shoulders and helped him toward the house. "Fetishes! The sorcerer!"

A crowd of children ran ahead. Others grouped around him. They chattered on. The sun had slid completely below the horizon, leaving only the brief moments of twilight.

"What's all this about?"

As they neared his house, Dominique heard his father's voice above the racket. He stumbled toward him. "The pastor's dog, Papa! It bit me!"

"And he's going to be crazy," one of the little girls piped up.

"Nonsense," returned his father. "Come in the house," he told Dominique. "And the rest of you go to your homes."

Dominique and his brothers told their father of their experience with the dog.

"And you boys had not been teasing?" he asked. "You were not doing anything you shouldn't?"

"No, Papa."

"Very well, we'll see. Come along. We are going to Pastor David's."

"But, Papa."

"You're not injured that badly. You can walk with me."

"But, Papa. It hurts." Dominique pressed the handkerchief more firmly against the gash, trying to ease the throbbing that had begun.

"You can walk."

Twilight gone, they carried a flashlight. "Pastor," his father asked when they arrived at the pastor's house, "was this boy or his brothers doing anything bad? Is that why your dog bit him?"

The pastor shook his head. "No. The dog likes to play. I never thought he would ever attack anyone. A thousand apologies. Me. A pastor . . . My dog . . ."

"Were the boys teasing?"

"No. Not at all."

"You're sure?"

"I'm sure. It was the dog. I never thought . . ."

"I'm satisfied if the boys were doing nothing wrong."

"I'll pay for the treatment."

Dominique's father shook his head. "It's not necessary, Pastor. I just wanted to make sure my boys were not causing you any trouble."

"I'm very sorry. It wasn't the boys," the pastor continued. "I've already tied the dog where he can be watched."

"I understand," Dominique's father broke in.

"Pastor David's a good man," Dominique said on their way home. "He could have blamed us. Instead he offered to pay.

"A man worthy of his calling," his father agreed.

They walked slowly through the night. The bright circle from the flashlight broke the darkness and guided them toward home. The throbbing in Dominique's back began to pulse with a burning pain, intense and frightening.

"Papa." A pleading whine tinged his voice. "Papa, I'm dying. Papa, hold me. I'm dying."

"What is it?" his father asked, putting an arm around his shoulder and drawing him close.

"My back. Oh, Papa. It hurts."

"You will be better."

"Papa . . ." Dominique felt more secure with his father's arm around him. With his closeness a bit of the pain seemed to drain away.

"What is it?"

"Will I be crazy?"

"Of course not!"

"But, Papa, they said . . ."

"There is a sickness that dogs can give people," his father admitted. "But only if the dogs have been sick themselves. That dog has not been sick."

"Papa."

"Yes?"

"What does it feel like to be crazy?"

"Son, you don't have to worry."

"But, Papa . . . "

"Yes?"

"They said that only strong fetishes and sorcerers can help against that sickness."

"You know what we have taught you."

"But I don't want to die."

"You have a future, son. The God in heaven will not let you die."

"But . . . How can I know? They said . . ."

"People say whatever comes into their heads," his father cautioned. "You can't listen to everything they say."

"But . . ."

"Remember the dream I told you about?"

"The dream about the road?"

"Yes, that one. I'll never forget it. A beautiful road, lighted and brilliant, stretched to the horizon. A man dressed in a white tunic stood in it, pointing. 'Follow this way,' he told me. In my heart I knew I must do as he said. The way of light, you know, is the way of God."

As his father spoke, Dominique noted the sound of conviction in his voice.

"My son, I want you, too, to follow the way of God. When we follow the way of God, we cannot mix His ways with the ways of darkness. God is stronger than fetishes or sorcery of any kind. You understand that, don't you?"

"Yes, Papa. I think I understand." They walked in silence for a few moments, then Dominique spoke again. "But, Papa, if you follow God's way, why don't you come to church with me?"

"That is a difficult question." His father spoke quietly, slowly. "Sometimes even the people of the church mix the light and the darkness."

"But the priest at the Catholic church is a good man, Papa. He speaks as a man of God."

"I am glad you go to his church, son. For me, though . . . I—I'm just not sure."

"It's a good church, Papa. They have lots of interesting things."

"I'm sure they do."

"When I went to school that first year, you should have seen the priest who came sometimes. He was a White man. And he had a beard—a huge, bushy brown beard. It went all the way down to the belt of his cassock. Papa, his beard was . . . it was absolutely amazing. It was thick and wavy and . . . I used to wait for him to come just so I could look at it."

His father chuckled. "Is that why you started going to church—just to look at a priest with a beard?"

"Papa . . ." Suddenly the realization of what he was saying caught up with him. "It was a *wonderful* beard." The two of them broke into laughter. "Not the beard!" he exclaimed when he found his voice again. "It's . . ." He became very serious. "It's the robes and the priests and the music and the altar and the dignity. It's . . ." His voice trailed away as he searched for words to explain his feelings.

"Is there something about the service that makes you feel almost as if you were coming into the presence of God?"

"Yes, Papa, yes. That's how it is." He wondered how his father had understood.

"Then continue in that way. It is important to follow the way that brings you to God. For me, I must find another way."

"Papa."

"Yes."

"My back still hurts."

"We will soon be home. Your mama will have hot water and warm cloths. They will ease the pain."

Dominique had a difficult time trying to find a comfortable spot in his bed that night. His back throbbed and pulsed with a fiery intensity. He twisted and turned in an effort to escape, but the pain would not let him go. At last he fell into a troubled sleep, but it seemed that dogs with big jaws full of pointed teeth kept darting at him. People lurking in the shadow laughed mockingly.

"Crazy! Crazy! Crazy!" they leered, pointing accusing fingers at him. "Festishers! Sorcerers!"

7

"Dominique! Dominique!"

At the sound of his name, Dominique turned. The pain in his back had kept him home from school several days, but the wound the dog had inflicted had healed by now, leaving only a lumpy scar as a reminder. The dog had shown no signs of rabies, thus erasing worries for his health. Fetishers and sorcerers were far from his thoughts.

"Dominique!"

Ilunga raced toward him, his bare feet pounding on the dusty path. As he neared, he slowed and fell into step with him. "Dominique, lend me your shoes."

Dominique stopped short at the abruptness of the demand. "You know I can't walk without them."

"Aw," wheedled Ilunga. "Just for a little while. I—I want to know how it feels to have shoes."

A smile flickered at the corners of Dominique's mouth. As almost the only ones in school with shoes, he and his little brothers sometimes engaged in a small commerce with them. For a cookie or a piece of candy, they would rent them out for a few moments. He looked keenly at Ilunga—Ilunga who could not possibly have anything to exchange. "OK." He spoke decisively. "I'll let you use my shoes. But you will have to carry me."

"It's a deal," Ilunga agreed quickly.

Dominique bent to unbuckle the brown sandals, while Ilunga stood expectantly to the side of the path. A look of satisfaction spread across Ilunga's face as he strapped on the shoes and stepped tentatively, testing their feel. "I'm ready!" he exclaimed. "Let's go!"

Dominique grasped his shoulders and jumped up to straddle his back. As they neared the school Ilunga slowed. "I'm getting tired," he admitted.

Dominique jumped down. "Business is business!" he exclaimed. "I'll have to have my shoes back."

The dry season stretched to the end of the school year, through the long holidays, and into the next school year. "Oh, Dominique," Kyungu complained one day. "Our shoes. We've already mended and remended them. And they just keep breaking."

"I know." Dominique looked thoughtful. "We do have enough saved now. The next time the cousin of my friend goes to Kaminaville, we can send the money with him. He'll buy our new shoes—and shirts and socks. And I want to get a new cloth for each of the mamas."

"Both of them?" Kabange asked. "Besides Mayombo's?"

"You know what Papa always says," Dominique reminded him. "When there are two mamas in the family, we must always treat them the same."

"Even if they do not always treat us as they should?"

"Shhh!" warned Dominique. "Both of our mamas are good to us."

"But it is not the same," complained Kabange. "We have our own mama. The other mama has only one sister for us."

"But she is still our mama, the wife of our papa. And we must show her respect as Papa has taught us. Papa wants us to have a family of peace."

"Peace!" snorted Kyungu, joining the argument. "With two mamas. Having to always pretend that they are both the same. Why did Papa have to marry two wives . . ."

"Shhh!" Dominique warned again. "Some papas have three and five and even more wives. It is the way of our ancestors."

"Sometimes I get tired of our ancestors. Mayombo is lucky. He has only one mama."

"Oh, Kyungu," remonstrated Dominique. "All this fuss just because you and Kabange want a new soccer ball from town. We still have the homemade one we got from the boys who live where the wild rubber trees grow. You can see our mama needs a new cloth. And you know it is not good for her to have a new one to wear if we do not get one for the other mama, too. We can always get a soccer ball later."

"But Tutu . . ."

"Kyungu."

"It is as you say."

Dominique gave the list of their order to the cousin of his friend and carefully counted out the money. After he left, the days could not pass fast enough for the boys. "When are our shoes coming?" Kabange demanded. "We've waited weeks and weeks already."

"The time is not yet," Dominique answered.

"But many trains have come already."

"It is not yet three weeks."

"When?"

"Another train will come tonight. Then the train that comes after three days." At last the day arrived. The sun dragged itself through that day and finally disappeared into the night. The night settled into a solid blackness with heavy clouds and no moon. The train was not due until eleven. Well before that time, Dominique, Kyungu, Kabange, and Mayombo were at the station. A flicker of light glowed from the kerosene lamp in the stationmaster's office. Before long a crowd gathered, milling about on the platform behind the barrier that kept them from the tracks.

"Hssst! I hear something!"

A momentary stillness whispered across the crowd, and in that instant Dominique could make out a faint vibrating rhythm. After a few moments, the sound grew more definite. Then the long wail of the train's whistle, followed by two shorter hoots, echoed through the night. Soon the platform vibrated with the heavy pulse of the giant engine and the clanking of its many iron wheels.

A confusion of "Wako-wako-wako-wako-wako-wako!" erupted as each person strained to shout a welcome louder than the others. People called from the station platform. People called from open carriage windows. People pressed toward the barrier. Dominique squeezed through the press and the noise to get as close to the entry as possible.

"Where are Pastor David's sons?" An urgent voice rose above the others.

"Pastor David's sons!" Their names rippled from voice to voice. Fragments of conversation broke above the general tumult. "There's been trouble. The pastor was thrown . . ."

Thoughts of shoes disappeared from Dominique's head as he strained to gather the pieces of the story.

"Bandits! The train didn't stop!"

"What?" Dominique wanted to shout. "What have they done with Pastor David?"

As the Kitenge passengers alighted, knots of people quickly formed around each one, everyone demanding at once to know what had happened. The stationmaster and his assistants held lanterns to aid those getting off. In the splash of light, Dominique saw his friend's cousin. He pushed himself farther through the milling crowd so he could be near when the cousin came through.

"Aa-uh, it's you, Dominique!" the man exclaimed. "I have all that you ordered. Tomorrow, when it's light, you can come to my house to get your things."

"Good!" Dominique responded. "But what are the people saying about Pastor David?"

The man shook his head. "It is terrible! Terrible, I tell you. We did not know what to do. It happened so quickly. Terrible!" he repeated.

By that time a small crowd had already formed itself about the man, trapping Dominique at his side. "Tell us!" demanded the others. "Tell us what happened!"

"Have the sons come?" the man asked.

"Someone has gone for them."

The man shook his head again. "I could not believe what was happening!" he exclaimed. "I was sitting just a few seats behind the pastor. He had been in Kamina the past weeks on church business. And he was happy to be on his way home. You know Pastor David, what a happy person he is, how he thinks of others. Well, when we got on the train before sunup this morning, he was there, encouraging the others about him, talking about the great God. And then he started singing songs of praise. You know how he can sing. And he had us all singing with him. We were having a good trip. Everyone felt good with a man like that to travel with."

"Yes . . . Yes . . . ," the crowd urged.

"Then . . . Just after the darkness . . . It was terrible . . . terrible."

Thinking of Pastor David, Dominique felt a tightness growing around his chest as he listened.

"Suddenly three men entered our coach, their faces dark and mean. They were dressed in the robes of the church, and the man in the center was carrying a Bible. He took one step forward. 'Silence!' he demanded.

"I can assure you that not one of us spoke. The very way the three of them had burst into our train car made us afraid. 'Our names are Jesus, Disciple, and Pastor,' the middle man continued. How terrible. Using the names of the church as he did. 'You are going to be silent!' he ordered. 'We are going to pray with you. And then!' He looked at us with an evil look. 'Then we are going to take up an offering.'

"We were stunned. Frightened. After the way Pastor David had been singing with us—then this!

"The man prayed. It was terrible. Then the ones he called Disciple and Pastor started coming down the aisle, demanding money from each person. We who travel the trains all know the dangers from the bandits who ride in these areas. We have heard many stories. Tonight we were the victims. We knew the three could not be alone, that they no doubt had helpers in our car. We did not dare but to do as they told us. When the so-called Pastor and Disciple came to the seat of our pastor . . ."

The man paused as if not sure just how to continue. "Pastor David pleaded with them to excuse him because he was a poor pastor with no money," he finally said. "While he was talking, trying to convince them, suddenly both Disciple and Pastor sprang at him. Grabbing him roughly, they hoisted him from his seat and shoved him out the window.

"People screamed. Women started crying. The train was

speeding through the brush country south of here. It was just past sundown. The man who called himself Jesus hollered in a terrible voice. 'If any of you so much as dares to move—or to speak—you, also, will be out there.'

"The car became deathly silent. The two men continued along the aisle, collecting money from everyone. And no one refused. Not knowing who among us might be their accomplices, we dared not move or speak. Not even after they left. The train sped on, the engineer not knowing that the pastor was back there somewhere along the track." The man shook his head again as if trying to shake away the thought. "Oh! It is so terrible. Pastor David must be dead."

Dominique felt all cold and tight inside. Pastor David, he thought miserably. Pastor David who was so good and so sorry when his dog bit me? Pastor David who held me and comforted me? That cannot be!

Already a group was forming at the far end of the platform. Several carried flashlights. In a splash of light Dominique saw two men carrying a bamboo litter. The women among them had already begun wailing the song of death. "Yo-yo-yo, yo-yo-yo," they repeated over and over. The men began to echo their wails. The cry rose louder and louder. They began moving along the tracks in the direction from which the train had come. Dominique started to follow.

"Shhhh!" someone commanded. "Stop your wails. We do not know if the pastor is truly dead. What will he think if he hears us coming like this?"

The people fell silent.

"We must hurry."

They all fell into a nearly running pace, taking long strides. Dominique dropped back. He could not follow them into the night. He must find his younger brothers and go home.

At home everyone was talking about what had happened. "How can bandits do wicked things like that, Papa?" Dominique demanded. "Pretending to be Jesus. Throwing good people off of the train."

"Greed and jealousy push men beyond reason," his father replied. "When our country gained independence, it was with the idea that all of our people would have a better life. There are those who want to be rich but do not want to work. In their greed they do many wicked things. Good people suffer. And the wicked become rich. But if you think, you will realize that the man who has gained his money wickedly can never have happiness. He will always have to be afraid, afraid that someday he will be caught and punished with a terrible punishment."

"But why?" Dominique insisted. "Why are people so wicked?"

"It is another of the ways of darkness. It is another way of the evil one to trap our people."

"Such people have no pure spirit," added Uncle Sondashi. "The prince of darkness has their hearts."

When Dominique finally got to bed, troubled thoughts chased through his mind. He thought of his father's dream, of the way of light. He thought of the sorcerers and fetishers and the evil ways in which they could trap people. He thought of the bandits who had no fear of harming others. And he wondered why so few chose the way of light. He had barely drifted off to sleep when a terrible noise filled his dreams. He lifted his head and realized that he was awake. The noise, loud and terrifying, continued. He jumped from his bed and ran to his mother's room. "Mama! Mama! What is that?" he demanded.

"Quiet, my boy. Quiet and listen." She pulled him down onto the bed beside her. "Isn't that the crying of people?" she asked gently. "Isn't that the wailing of the people when death has come? Isn't it that Pastor David is dead?"

In solemn silence Dominique listened. The sounds from the night began to distinguish themselves. He heard the "Yo-yo-yo. Yo-yo-yo. E-i-e. Ta-ta. Ta-ta." They were the sounds of sadness, the loud wailing of mourning, the calling for a father who has died. "Then it is true that the pastor is dead?"

"I'm afraid that is so."

"That is very sad, Mama."

"Very sad," she repeated.

"Pastor David was a good man," he said quietly.

"Yes. A man who represented well the God of his faith."

"Someday I want to be a man of God like Pastor David," Dominique said suddenly.

"Your papa and I want you to be a good man."

"Should we go to the pastor's house to give our condolences to the family?" he asked.

"That is the way it should be done," replied his mother. "Since we are not of his family nor of his church, we can better wait until the morning. Go. Try to sleep. You will need strength because it will be a sad day."

In the morning there was no thought of racing to get the new shoes. Instead Dominique went in the manner of a true friend to give his condolences to the grieving family. As his mother had said, it was a sad day. School was closed. No one went to the fields. Most gathered to mourn with the family. After visiting them, Dominique and his brothers went to get their things. Then, wearing the new shoes, they went back to the house of Pastor David and followed the great crowd to church for the services of interment. An old pastor from the next village had come to preach.

"Our beloved Pastor David has suffered a brutal death," he began. "You have no doubt all heard the story of how on the way back from Kamina yesterday he was singing the praises of God. It is, you could say, as if he knew he was going to die and that he was preparing his heart for God."

Dominique listened carefully.

"In the same way, I am asking each of you to have faith in God, to believe His word, to trust in Him, so that you may prepare your hearts for God. Pastor David gave his life for the gospel. He wanted you, his people, to have faith. Now, in his place, I am asking you to follow his example."

The words of the old preacher reached into Dominique's heart. "Have faith?" he asked himself. "How can I have faith?"

8 "You shouldn't talk to everyone like that about the boy."
Dominique knew he was not meant to overhear his other
mother as she scolded his father. "Someone could do him harm."

"The boy is intelligent," his father argued. "He will study far
away. He is not always going to remain here in the village."

"People laugh when you say that."

"It is not a laughing matter," retorted his father. "I am serious.
That boy will study."

"How can you talk like that about the boy of a wife of no
importance."

Dominique could hear the scorn creeping into his other
mother's voice. "How can you talk of him going far away to study
when our own daughter has never seen the inside of a school."

"It is different with our girl. She is a girl of the village. She will make some man a good wife. She is worth a good dowry. But the boy is a boy of the future." His father spoke with conviction. "I have arranged with my sister. He will go to live with her in Elisabethville."

Dominique slipped away from the house and went to the workshop. The twins were busy cutting bamboo into proper lengths for the two cars they were building. "By the time school starts again we'll have lots of cars built!" exclaimed Kabange. "We have lots of bamboo in stock. With the holidays . . ."

"Mmmmmuhm," agreed Dominique absentmindedly. "We'll have lots of time." But his thoughts were far away from their thatched workshop, far away from their railroad village of mud-brick and thatch houses.

"Dominique!" The sound of his father's voice brought him back to reality. "Dominique! Come!"

"Yes, Papa." He hurried to where his father was sitting beside the house in the shade of the roof overhang.

"Dominique. We need to talk about your future."

"Yes, Papa."

"About your school. If you are to continue with secondary school, it is not good that you have only attended a simple village school like ours. It would be better if you went away to the city to study at one of the big schools."

Dominique pulled a bamboo stool close to his father and sat down, waiting for him to continue.

"I have written a letter to my sister who lives with her husband in Elisabethville. She has said that you can go to live with her to finish your schooling."

"To Elisabethville, Papa?"

"It is better for your future to study there. You will go in time to be there when the new term begins."

So it was that on the first day of September, Dominique found himself on the train, heading toward Elisabethville. For the first hours, the train sped through the rolling, forest-patched, river-laced savanna. They had long passed the area of Pastor David's accident, and the excitement of going to live in the city held back any somber memories from his thoughts. Instead as he watched the countryside slip by, his thoughts roamed the forests. Once again he was hunting with his little brothers. He remembered the snake he had killed. He remembered the huge elephant that had fallen before the mighty hunter. And the words of the hunter came back to him: "The wise person goes to more than one market. In order to do well with your studies, you must be like the military. It takes courage to find success."

"I am traveling to my future. I have courage. But . . ." He wondered about Elisabethville. He wondered if studies in a city school would be more difficult. He knew that his father was one of the few people back home in Kitenge with a sixth-grade diploma. He had even passed the secondary preparatory year and had wanted to go on. He had lacked the means, though, and instead had gone to work for the Belgians. Dominique wondered if he would do as well, if he would pass his sixth-year examinations as his father had. His father's parting words came back to him. "You are a child of the future. I am counting on you to do well."

"I will do my best," he promised himself. "I will do my best."

The train rolled on toward the hills to the south, through them, and on toward the city. As they reached the outskirts of Elisabethville, Dominique marvelled at the seemingly unending stretches of houses. Then, as they moved farther into town, he stared in open-mouthed wonder at the tall buildings—like many houses stacked one on top of the other. Roofs were not thatched, but covered with red or gray tiles. When the train reached the station, his aunt and uncle were waiting for him.

"How can someone build such houses?" he asked his uncle after their greetings were over. "What intelligence! What wisdom!"

"Such knowledge comes from studies, my boy," his uncle replied.

Dominique continued to stare upwards in amazement. "Buildings many houses high," he repeated. "With such things, how can I ever be discouraged about learning?"

The year passed quickly. Dominique found that he could do just as well in the city as in the village. School hours were the same, with classes finished by twelve-thirty each day. His uncle, a mechanic with one of the government firms, set him up in a small business selling candies and cookies at the street corner in front of his house. Business was good. He developed several regular customers, and gradually his savings mounted.

Almost before he knew it, the last day of school had come. His aunt and uncle went with him to proclamation, the presentation of certificates. "Dominique Kalumba," the headmaster called at last.

"Third in a class of 71."

Cheers and applause filled the room as Dominique went forward to receive the certificate that said he had completed his elementary studies with distinction. "Dominique," whispered his uncle when he had come back to his place, "we're proud of you! Just wait until your papa sees that certificate!"

Dominique could hardly wait for that. The following Monday his uncle took him to the station. His big valise was loaded with presents. New shoes for his younger brothers, for the first time in real leather, and a real soccer ball. Clothes for his parents. But most important, in a big envelope at the bottom of the valise, where it could not be lost, was his precious certificate.

The waiting room was packed with students—all on their way to their home villages for the school holidays. When the train was announced at last, Dominique crowded on with the others. He had reservations in the sleeping compartment for the two-day trip. He stowed the large valise on the luggage rack, along with his shoulder bag that his aunt had packed with a lunch for the journey and his bag filled with handicrafts he had bought from a street vendor for decorating his room at home. He settled in for the long trip. The train rolled northward. In the heavy warmth he felt drowsy, but his excited thoughts would not let him sleep. He leaned his head against the window, contented. "Papa will be happy," he told himself. "I have proved his faith in me."

Station after station marked their progress toward the north. The train pulled into yet another station. Night had already fallen. From far away it seemed that he heard someone knocking. Then he heard it louder. Someone was knocking at the window across from where he was sitting.

"Aay! You rebel!" called out one of the boys ahead of him. "What are you doing knocking on our window?"

In the next instant a huge roar seemed to fill the compartment. Dominique stared toward the door. A hefty soldier, red faced, shoved himself in and hulked in the aisle. "Who insulted me?" he shouted. "You! Why have you insulted me?" He glowered menacingly at one of the boys.

"Sorry. Excuse us," spoke up an older student in the first seat. "We did not realize it was you."

The big soldier continued to glower. "If you don't tell who insulted me, you'll be sorry," he warned.

No one spoke. No one moved. Dominique tried to look as unimportant as possible.

"If you don't tell," the soldier bellowed, "your baggage will be held."

Dominique felt a sudden panic seize him. Baggage? The presents! My certificate! His mind raced wildly.

The soldier stomped out of the compartment. The sigh of relief that started to escape Dominique quickly stopped when the man suddenly reappeared with a whole group in military uniform. All had been on leave and were returning to a military base far to the north.

"You!" the first exclaimed, jabbing his finger at the chest of one of the boys across from Dominique. "Why did you insult us? We want to know the reason."

The boy shook his head, unable to speak.

The soldier pointed at another.

"I didn't—" he started to say.

"Then who did?" he barked.

No one spoke.

"All right. You don't want to talk. Then we'll teach you who you can insult." The soldiers began moving down the aisle, slapping at the boys. One swung his fist at Dominique. Involuntarily, Dominique ducked and the fist topped his head.

"How's that?" the soldier demanded, leering toward him. "You don't want to tell. You'll lose your things," he sneered. "You'll be put off."

Dominique recoiled from the blow and stared up tight-mouthed. All the happiness of a few minutes before had vanished, and in its place was a terrible fear. My valise! he thought frantically. My certificate! If it was lost, he knew according to law he would never be given another. Without an elementary certificate he could never be accepted into secondary school.

"Put these fellows out of this compartment," ordered the first soldier. "We know who will be glad for these places, don't we?" He laughed a hollow laugh. "You!" he pointed to one of his buddies. "Guard the baggage so they don't get any bright ideas."

Before the soldier could say anything more, Dominique was on his feet, scampering back through the corridor to the third-class section. He tried to become inconspicuous in a crowded car where there was only standing room.

"Where are you going?" a gruff voice behind him asked.

"Me?" Dominique demanded, startled. Then, catching himself, he named a station far beyond Kitenge.

"Go back to your compartment!"

Dominique tried not to show his surprise and quickly made his way back. As silently as possible, he slipped into his seat. A soldier still stood sullenly guarding the luggage rack, not speaking. A few soldiers sat in the compartment in place of the boys they had chased out, but most of them had disappeared.

The kilometers clicked off under the train wheels but the rails no longer sang. Dominique's stomach knotted with worry. "God," he prayed over and over, "how can I get my things back?"

9 As the train rolled into another night and then into the next day, Dominique continued to mull over his problem. "How?" he demanded of himself. "How can I get that heavy valise out of here?" He looked across at a man who had boarded in Kamina. He seemed familiar. He was sure he had seen him in Kitenge before. "If that soldier would just leave," he told himself, "maybe I could do something."

The train began to slow for Kitenge station. As if reading Dominique's thoughts, the soldier turned from the luggage rack and headed toward the rear of the train. From the commotion in the back, Dominique knew people were hurling their belongings out the windows as far as possible beyond the tracks. The man across the aisle stood and began to collect his baggage. Dominique's shoulders sagged. He wished he dared to do the same, but never could he hoist that heavy valise to heave to safety. Suddenly an idea seized him.

"If you go outside," he suggested, going to the man, "I could hand your things out—and mine. You could put them by the fence."

"Excellent idea, boy!" exclaimed the man. Instantly he was off the train and running along the open window.

An eye alert for the soldier, Dominique worked quickly. By the time he had struggled his valise out, the train had screeched to a full stop. He dashed to the door and jumped, anxious to hurry his things to the station. Instead, he stopped short. His three bags had been left together right by the train. Beside them stood the soldier who had been insulted—and a buddy.

"What shall I do now?" he asked himself, heart sinking. "If I don't show myself, my things will certainly disappear. If I do . . ." He stood there pondering his situation. "I have to have that certificate," he decided desperately. "No matter what, I have to have it." He advanced toward his bags—and the soldiers.

"Who do these belong to?" The first soldier folded his arms methodically across his chest and faced Dominique squarely.

"Big Brother," Dominique replied politely, using Lingala, the language of the military. "Big Brother, they are for me."

"Oh? For you! The one who insults!"

"Excuse me, Big Brother. I am innocent. I do not know what you are talking about."

"Because you insult the military, I will take these along." The soldier clipped his words with cold precision.

"But, Big Brother, I am innocent."

"Then you must show me the one."

Dominique sensed more than saw the townspeople standing just beyond the barrier that separated the rails from the platform. Behind him he could hear a chatter of welcome blending with other voices hawking wares. "Please, Big Brother, I do not know the one who insulted you." He forced himself to speak with politeness.

The soldier opened his right hand broadly and purposefully pulled back his arm.

Dominique, staring at the solid form, knew that with his skimpy not quite 14 years of growth, he could never withstand such a blow. He ducked quickly and felt the hand whistle above his hair.

"Aaa-aah! So he wants to amuse me!" cried the soldier. His second blow exploded broadside across Dominique's ear. Dominique felt the ear pop, and the noise from the idling train disappeared from that side of his head.

"My friend." The second soldier spoke for the first time. "Leave the little one."

"The impudent little upstart," retorted the first.

"Let him go," advised his friend. "If he was my little brother, would you treat him like that?"

"Mmmmphh!"

"Well . . ."

"Aaahh . . . OK! Go on, runt. Get out of here with your things." With his boot, he kicked Dominique's valise.

"Thank you, Big Brother." Dominique quickly grabbed up his bag and slung its strap over his shoulder. With the sack in one hand, he dragged the heavy valise with the other, anxious to pass through the opening in the barrier before the soldier could be seized with another spasm of anger. Head down, he forced himself toward the platform, not daring to stop. He hurried as fast as he could, but the platform planks did not seem solid under his feet. He struggled to keep his balance. One side of his head felt big and numb.

"Tutu! Tutu! Wako-wako-wako-wako-wako-wako . . ."

The twins and Mayombo rushed at him, crying their welcome and pounding his shoulders all at the same time.

"Eyo Vidye. Eyo Vidye" ("Yes, Eternal One"), Dominique forced himself to speak the proper words to each one individually in the manner of the Luba. His father had taught him that one must always respond with respect, for no matter who greeted him, that person stood before him in the place of God, a neighbor to be loved as one must love God. But his head! It jarred dully with the exuberance of the boys' greetings. He could hear nothing on the one side.

"What is it?" demanded Kyungu, pulling back and regarding his older brother. "Tutu, we did not know you would be on this train, not until the others came to tell us. They said the soldiers hit you. Why?"

Dominique shrugged. "Such things happen," he evaded, not wanting to explain. "My ear is stopped. Before I talk, I must first get my ear back."

The boys grabbed up his things and led the way up the hill toward their place. Dominique stumbled dizzily after them. The heat of the midafternoon sun burned down. When they arrived, his mother rushed about to get a pot of water onto the cooking fire. While she worked, she made Dominique sit on his father's chair under the edge of the roof away from the heat of the sun. "Before you talk, you must wash," she insisted. "I will make the water as hot as it can be made, for a cloth that you will put across your ear."

When the water was ready he went into the house to wash. The hot cloth felt good against his ballooning head. His body relaxed as he washed away the dirt from the two days on the train. He took his time soaking, enjoying, but at the same time worrying. Suddenly something whistled out of his ear and he felt a noise. Then he could hear. "E-e-e-e-e-e-e-e-e-e!" he screamed, jumping up.

"What is it?" His mother's voice at the door sounded anxious.

"There is something hidden that I will show you," he responded, using a Kiluba proverb. "Just as soon as I come out." Going out, he felt like a new person. "I have my ear back, Mama!" he exclaimed. "I have my ear back . . . and it's good to be home!"

His father, who had been away, did not arrive until later that evening. "If I'd been there," he exclaimed angrily upon hearing the story, "If I'd been there . . ."

"It's good that you weren't," responded his younger brother, Uncle Sondashi. "The boy got himself out of the scrape. If you had started something, matters could have become grave."

As Dominique listened to the men, his thoughts took a different turn. "God gave me the courage," he told himself. "Don't worry, Papa," he said aloud. "I am here and I can hear as good as always."

His father smiled. "That is good and we are glad to have you with us again." He stood up. "Come with me," he invited, "I have something to show you."

Dominique followed his father to the little building behind the house. The two of them went in. When his eyes adjusted to the dim light, he saw a big ram tethered to the support pole in the middle of the room and several chickens. His father reached down and began purposefully to stroke the head of the ram. "Son," he began, "we are indeed very happy to see you here again, very happy and very proud of your success." He continued to pet the ram, but he carefully avoided looking at it. Instead he faced around to look steadily at Dominique. "Because of this, in the name of all the family, we have kept something for you."

As Dominique stood before his father looking up at him, he realized the importance of the moment. He felt a surge of honor, a sense of the pride of his Luba people, and in that moment it seemed that he stood at the threshhold of growing up.

"We are just poor village people and we cannot do everything for you that we would like in order to show our love and our happiness in your accomplishments. Just the same, our people have their ways of showing honor and satisfaction in their children. We want you to have something you will always remember. And we have kept this ram for you—a fine, healthy animal, as you can see, with no sickness or blemishes. Many people will be coming to celebrate your success with us. If you wish, our guests may feast tonight."

Dominique reached out to lay his right hand on the ram, for one must always accept a gift with the hand of the arm of force. "Wafwako ["Thank you"], Papa." He bowed respectfully, his eyes fixed on the earthen floor. "Thank you for this honor that you are showing me." He too began to stroke the soft fur, and he turned his head to face his father. "I know that one cannot give a better gift, a gift of more importance or that shows greater appreciation, than that of a live animal. Thank you," he repeated again. "Thank you very much. Tell the mama to care for it," he added, using the Kiluba expression that would let his father know that it should be prepared for the feast.

"There are also these chickens." His father picked up one of the hens in his two hands and held it toward Dominique. "I want you to see that we have chosen well. These are large and healthy."

Dominique reached out to receive the chicken with his two hands, as one should do for small gifts that can he held. "Wafwako, Papa. I see that this is a fine hen." He hefted it as if trying to judge its weight. "And big." He spoke a few more words in its praise, then set it back on the floor and reached out to receive each of the others as his father presented them in turn. "We will save these for later."

At dusk the people began filling the palm-branch enclosure his father had built for the occasion. Nothing would do but that

Dominique be brought in the style of a traditional king, in the style that showed he was no longer a person of ordinary rank. His oldest sister, the daughter of his other mother, occupied the position of privilege. Carrying Dominique on her back, followed by the younger sisters, brothers, and cousins, she led the triumphal entry into the crowded enclosure and placed Dominique on the chair of honor. The younger ones found places to sit nearby on the ground. When they were seated, Dominique's father entered, carrying his gun.

"If I shoot into the sky," he announced, aiming toward the heavens, "it is a visa for my son." He snapped off the safety catch and fired. "The bullet goes quickly," he continued, "but it comes back. Our people have the saying that an arrow shot into the sky is on a promenade, but that the earth is its lodging. It is the same with a son who travels far and learns much. He must not forget his family."

He went over to Dominique and took his hand. "Courage, my son," he said. "All of this, your primary certificate, is a good beginning. We hope that what we have shot into the sky has given you a stronger idea about continuing your studies. What you are learning is not only for you—it is for everyone. You will have surprises because of your studies, surprises that will demand courage. Wherever they take you, never forget this bullet that has gone into the sky and returned. Never forget your family, your home, or your people."

The big moon began its trip into the tropical sky, giving the night a silvery softness and gently lighting the courtyard. After the speeches, Dominique's big cousin started playing his accordian. The drummers joined in and the singing and feasting and dancing began. The moon passed its zenith. "You must go to bed," Dominique's father urged him.

"I'm happy to be home, to be with you. Let me stay."

"But you have had a long trip. You need to rest."

Reluctantly Dominique went to his room. He lay down but sleep would not come. As he lay staring up into the moon-softened darkness, he wondered about his future. Papa says my studies are not just for me but for everyone, he pondered. But how . . . ?

Neither sleep nor an answer would come. At last he went out again. The women were busy stoking up the fires to reheat the food. Already the gold of another sun reached into the sky of the morning. His father stood to speak to the guests. The music stopped.

"Thank you to all of you who have come to celebrate the success of our Dominique," he began. "He has brought home his primary certificate from Elisabethville. When September comes he will be back there in secondary school. Me. I had no chance to continue my studies. But now . . . Now a new time has come. The government is building schools, and it is important for our children to study. You see the development of the world, and you, children, if you will learn, our own area will develop.

"Now we have difficulties we cannot solve—difficulties regarding food and clothes and work. Studies help us to find answers to these problems. You children, we will help you. We will encourage you. But you are the ones who must study. The one who does not study is at the mercy of his own caprices. He cannot develop as he should, for studies have a big role in our development.

"Our future, our tomorrow, is with our children. I have fought for my son to study. I want to encourage all of you to help your children to study. It is important for all of us."

Dominique stood at his father's side. His father looked down at him and he knew what he must do. "Thank you to all of you who have come to this feast in my honor," he began. "I am happy to be home. I thank you for coming to welcome me. I thank you for your encouragement.

"I know you have children like me. You must continue to encourage us. We children cannot do anything without the encouragement of our parents. If it were not for the encouragement of my papa and my mama, I would not have continued with school. When I began, I did not like school. I did not see the value of it. I wanted to stay at home and hunt with my little brothers. I felt our future lay in the forest.

"But Papa explained how our world is changing. He told me that our future will consist of more than hunting the animals of the forest and of the savanna.

"I have seen the mighty elephant killed by one of our powerful hunters. I have seen the large antelope trapped by the craft of my grandfather. Now I have been to the city. I have seen the buildings that are many houses tall. I have seen the big houses and I have lived in the big house of my aunt—a house with many rooms, so that each child may have his own. A house with pipes coming in, so that with a turn of a knob, water comes into a basin for washing and bathing and cooking and drinking. A house that has wires coming with power that makes the light of many candles at night and chases the darkness, so we can read and study and do our other work. I have seen the vehicles and the clothes and the machines that make life more comfortable.

"I have also seen that it is the person who studies that has the knowlege to make these things, and he will have work so that he may earn to buy these things.

"We, your children, do not yet have the experience to understand all of this. But if you, our mamas and papas, will help us, we will have the courage to continue our studies. We will have the courage to prepare ourselves for the future. Now we are not experienced. But with your encouragement, with your help, with the will of God, that experience will come. We will continue little by little. Our studies are the preparation that we need."

The holidays swept by as if they were on the wings of a big bird. The time neared for Dominique to return to Elisabethville.

"Dominique!"

Dominique saw his father standing with a letter in his hand. He looked serious. "Your aunt has written. She says you are not to come back to stay with her."

Dominique stared at his father in shocked silence. "She what . . . ?" he faltered.

"She says you are not to come back to stay with them. Do you know anything about this?"

Dominique shook his head.

"Sometimes I do not understand my sister." His father sighed.

"What will I do?" When the full realization of what his father was saying struck him, he almost shouted the question. "Where will I stay?"

10 "Ngoy [N-go-ee], I'm worried." Plunging his hands deeply into the pockets of his uniform trousers, Dominique trudged beside his friend. "I wish I could find another place to stay."

"Doesn't your sister want you?"

"Not that. My sister, Ngongo, is fine. It's Malela, her husband."

"What's the problem?"

"Fish."

"Fish?"

A discouraged half-laugh escaped Dominique. "Yes, fish." He sighed. "You know the job I have—unloading fish into cold storage early every morning. I'm paid in fish—six big ones every day. I sell three to get money for school. I take three home."

"What's wrong with that?"

"Malela complains because we have to eat fish every day."

"Then don't bring any home."

"If I sell them and give my sister the money to buy something else, he's afraid I'm cheating them."

"I'm glad my papa found a good place for me to stay. The people are satisfied with the money he pays every month."

"Your papa works for the government. My papa . . ." Dominique paused. "He worked for the Belgians before independence. In the tax department. With the war, he had to flee back to the village. He works, but it is not the same anymore. Now we're just people of the village."

Ngoy nodded. "I understand. And our papas want us in school in the city, where we'll have to be serious. I begged my papa to let me stay home, but he said, 'No. If you're home, we'll spoil you too much. Go to the city. There you'll have to be serious.'"

"Serious, that's for sure," Dominique agreed. "They're talking of building a secondary school back home in Kitenge. Papa won't hear of me going home, though, for the same reason. African families have a habit of spoiling their children who study, he says."

The boys walked on toward their school, silent for a few moments. "About now I could use just a little bit of spoiling," Dominique began again. "Last year I had it good with my aunt. I was looking forward to going back to her place. But she refused. Her boys did not do as well in school as I did. You know how it is—the jealousies. Now . . ." He kicked at a pebble lying on the sidewalk. "My sister's happy to have me, but she's only a couple years older than I am, hardly 16. She's been married only a few months and lives with her husband in a little two-room apartment. And then there's me—and her husband's two brothers."

"Life can have its complications," Ngoy interjected sympathetically.

"The doves! Ha! The doves!"

The two boys spun around.

"Look at the pretty white doves!"

"Just you stay out of our way!" yelled Ngoy, shaking his fist at their taunters.

"The doves," Dominique repeated sarcastically under his breath. "To make life more complicated we had to choose a school with all-white uniforms."

"Let them tease," consoled Ngoy. "It's a good school."

Another of their classmates came out of a side street to join them. "I need you to talk to your brother," he said, falling into step with Dominique. "My math grade . . ."

"The math teacher is not my brother," Dominique objected.

"Don't tell me that," argued the boy. "Anyone can tell by looking that he's your brother. And notice how he favors you. Everyone knows you get the best grades."

"I tell you, he is not my brother. I never before saw the man until I began school this year."

"You just don't want to help me."

"I tell you . . ."

"Aw, come on." The boy's voice took on a wheedling tone. "Period exams are coming. I don't stand a chance, but I need to pass." He reached into his pocket. "See this jackknife," he continued, holding out his hand. "You talk to your brother and it's yours."

"That's not my fashion," Dominique returned, annoyance creeping over him. "Keep your knife. I cannot help you. The man is not my brother. Even if he were . . ."

"Tssssh!" the boy hissed, spinning on his heel. "You just don't want to help me!"

Dominique watched him disappear. "Complications!" he spluttered to Ngoy. "Just because I look like the man, they try to pay me to get good grades for them."

"I thought you were brothers at first too."

"This business of trying to buy me . . . If they want grades, let them work."

"That's not always the way."

"What good are grades without knowledge?"

"To get a diploma."

"Then why go to school?"

"I sometimes ask myself that very question." Ngoy laughed. "I hear you can buy a good-looking diploma from any school you want—if you know the right people."

"I've heard that too." Dominique shook his head. "I don't understand . . ."

"You know how some people are," Ngoy replied. "Our ancestors were clever in the ways of deceit. These today think that deceit will bring them success in this new life too."

The school stood just around the corner. The warning whistle sounded. Both boys broke into a run.

"I have a very important announcement," their homeroom teacher began when everyone was settled in class. "As you know, the government, to give a sense of authenticity to our heritage, has already changed the name of our country from the Democratic Republic of the Congo to the Republic of Zaire. The name of our city was changed from Elisabethville to Lubumbashi."

Dominique wondered what the teacher was leading up to.

"We have become accustomed to these new names. Now the government is asking us to make one more change, a change to help us feel more proud of being Zairois. We are all being asked to choose authentic Zairois names—names that have belonged to our ancestors. All of us with foreign names and those of us who have been named after Christian saints are being asked to choose new names."

Dominique listened in surprise. "A new name?" he asked himself.

"In addition," continued the teacher, "we will begin to address each other as 'citoyen' for the men and 'citoyenne' for the ladies. No longer will we use 'monsieur' or 'madame' or 'mademoiselle.' That was the style of the colonists and from now on will be used only to address the strangers visiting our country.

"All of you will need to discuss this matter with your parents and to choose good, authentic names that have belonged to your families in the past. After the Christmas holidays you will be required to register your new names."

"Well, what do you think of this change?" Ngoy asked after classes that afternoon.

Dominique shook his head. "I like my name; it's the name of my father. You're lucky. You already have a traditional name."

"Ngoy? But my ID papers will have to be changed. My legal name is Charles Ngoy."

"What new name will you choose?"

"I don't know. I'll talk with my papa during holidays."

"I won't be going home," Dominique said thoughtfully. "It's not an easy matter to give oneself a new name—a good name."

Ngoy turned off at his street and Dominique walked the next blocks lost in thought. "Complications," he muttered, automatically making his way toward his sister's place. He turned into an alley. "A new name?" Passing the third house, he crossed into the path that led through the courtyard with the public water tap, that separated the house where his sister lived from the neighbors. A crowd milled about. He pushed through them. Something white flying out of the door caught his attention. Startled, he stopped. Ngongo, his sister, sat on her stone porch step, head in hands. Strewn on the red-brown earth before her were an open valise and clothes. Dominique stared, his brain trying to register comprehension. "My clothes?" he was asking himself. A wadded ball flew out the door and opened into another shirt. It fluttered to the earth in front of him. His jaw went slack.

"Of all the nerve!" The indignant voice of their neighbor sounded behind him. "Sending the boy out just like that. It's not right." She brushed past him and began picking up the clothes.

Dominique watched dumbly as the woman gathered his things. He looked at his sister hunched on the step. On impulse he headed past them and into the house. He could hear Malela inside, beyond the curtain. He paused by the table. A large piece of paper stared up at him with his name scrawled across the top. He picked it up. "Dominique," he read. "From this day I do not want to see you in this house. Malela."

He folded the paper neatly, put it in his pocket, and turned toward the door. He strode purposefully out without an idea of where he was going. As he stepped off the stoop, he heard his sister get up behind him.

"Pardon," she called after him. "Pardon."

He paused.

"Pardon," she repeated. "It is not what I wanted."

"Why?" he demanded.

Ngongo lowered her eyes. "We are young. We have no children."

"I will go," he said flatly. "I do not want to cause you any more difficulties."

"But where?"

He turned and hurried away without replying.

11

"I see you have solved the problem of your name!" Ngoy exclaimed, catching up with Dominique after class.

"My father took care of that—by letter. What a day! New names! Presents from the government—books, pens, notebooks! We've got a good country! We can forget we were ever colonized!"

"Long live Zaire!" Ngoy called, raising his arm in triumph.

"Long live Zaire!" Dominique echoed. "Long live Zaire—the country with a future!" Suddenly he stopped and faced his friend. "Ngoy." His tone was serious. "Today really is the first day of a new beginning, isn't it?"

"Yes, Kongolo." Ngoy smiled lopsidedly at the strange feel as he pronounced the new name for the first time. "Yes, Citoyen Kongolo who used to be Dominique. Today we have new names.

Today every one of us has received a gift of new school things from the government. Today is the first day of a new future."

"I wonder if everyone feels the change we feel."

Ngoy looked thoughtful but said nothing.

"I mean . . . Well, today I have become Kongolo Kalumba Wa Muhunga-Nday. Oh, surely the family and others may continue to call me by my ex name, Dominique, But now, me, I am Kongolo. I have the name of our ancient king—a name that means 'rainbow—a promise.' And I have the names of my father and my father's father. I feel that there is something special about the future—something very special that also has a lot to do with our past."

"Kongolo, I think I know what you mean."

The late afternoon sun beat down hot, very hot. On the eastern horizon, above the rooftops, massive thunderheads billowed into the deep blue. A slight breeze began to stir. The clouds seemed to balloon toward each other, their innocent white quickly churning into an angry gray.

"We'd better run!" Ngoy exclaimed suddenly. "The rain!"

The boys broke into long strides. Thunder growled ominously as the storm unleashed itself on the other side of the city in typical rainy-season fashion. They ran faster.

Kon-go-lo. Kon-go-lo. Kon-go-lo. The syllables bounced through his mind, reinforced with each footfall. I am Kon-go-lo. By the time he had reached Papa Fwelema's, where he had been staying since the day Malela had chased him from his house, fat, tepid raindrops began to slap down. He was barely inside when the torrent broke loose and thrashed against the tile roof. Lightning flared across the sky, and thunder roared overhead.

During the next weeks, storms punctuated the torrid temperatures almost daily. Sometimes laced violently with thunder and lightning, sometimes soft and monotonous, the rain might be over in a matter of minutes or it might settle in for hours and hours. Whichever the case, afterward the skies cleared into a brilliant blue studded with cloud puffs, and the sun quickly dried the earth.

One morning the new Kongolo (Dominique), hurrying back to Papa Fwelema's after his job of unloading fish, heard a loud voice calling in the next street. Curious, he paused. "The person who has stolen my belongings must announce himself." The voice carried an ominous quality. "He must announce himself within four days. Otherwise, on the fifth day . . ."

Kongolo shivered involuntarily. He heard the voice calling again, this time from farther away. "What . . . ?" he started to ask himself, then his father's old warning came to mind. "Avoid that which you do not understand." He hurried on. "I will talk with Papa Fwelema when I have opportunity," he told himself. "He understands. I can trust him."

"Aah, yes," replied Papa Fwelema when they were alone in the living room after supper that evening. "You have heard the voice of a messenger for the 'lancer de foudre.' "

"Lancer de foudre?"

"The sorcerer who has power to call the lightning to strike someone," explained Papa Fwelema.

"Here?"

"Even in the city. Even in these modern times," replied the old man. "Many people ignore the teachings of the Bible. They continue in the ways of our ancestors. They use the evil power of the sorcerers to mete out justice."

"What will happen?" asked Kongolo.

"In the tradition of our people, the one who was robbed goes to the sorcerer to buy punishment for the thief. Yet even in this practice of darkness, there is some justice, but only because the person may get his things back. A messenger must be sent throughout the area. For three days he gives warning that the thief must confess, specifying the day of punishment. If by that day the one robbed has not been contacted, he will go again to the sorcerer.

"And lightning will be called down upon the thieves?" Kongolo asked.

"Only God is stronger than these powers of darkness."

The two of them sat in silence a moment, then Kongolo spoke. "Every night I pray that God will protect me. Every morning I pray that He will give me wisdom for the day."

"God will be with you," Papa Fwelema replied gently. "God will be with you."

The next two mornings Kongolo again heard the messenger. On the afternoon of the fifth day another storm lashed furiously at the city. The next morning knots of people collected here and there in the street. "Six people," he overheard someone saying.

"Ten people sitting together in a room. Six struck."

Kongolo paused on the edge of the crowd.

"With the signs of the sorcerer too," another added.

"Their tongues . . . gone."

"The thieves, for sure."

Kongolo listened silently, taking in the details but not joining the conversation.

"The lightning pushed aside the four innocent," another inserted. "But the six guilty—all dead. The ways of the sorcerer are sure."

But the God in heaven is stronger, Kongolo reassured himself, moving away from the crowd and continuing on his way.

12

For his third year of secondary school, Kongolo lived again with his sister. Returning one evening, he saw another crowd of neighbors milling about the door. His stomach knotted with apprehension. Not again! he moaned inwardly, hoping that his suspicions might be unfounded. He worked his way through the bystanders. There by the doorstep, in a jumbled heap, his clothes and books awaited him. Clamping his teeth together hard, he grabbed his valise from where it tilted haphazardly against the foundation stones and began stuffing in his things. Finished, he slammed it shut and hoisted it to his shoulder. Without a word he set off with long, heavy strides. He walked with determined steps, as if he knew exactly where he was going. The heavy suitcase dug into his shoulder.

"Kongolo!"

At the sound of his name he paused involuntarily, then caught himself and hurried on.

"Kongolo!"

The insistence of the voice cut through to his senses. He paused and half turned.

"Kongolo! Wherever are you going?" Shabami, a good friend from school, hurried toward him.

"I don't know."

"You don't know?" Shabami caught up with him. "Do you mean . . . ?"

Kongolo let the heavy valise slide to the sidewalk. "He's done it again." Suddenly all of the energy seemed to drain from his body, and he sank down to sit on his valise.

"But I thought you said he promised . . ."

"Promises." Kongolo cupped his chin in his hands and stared down at the curb. "After that first time, when he came with all his apologies, begging me to come back, my parents thought I should try it my second year. You know how long that lasted—till the middle of the year. Then back to Papa Fwelema's. Now, this year. There were more apologies, more pleading, more promises. They moved to a new apartment in a new section of town. I'm in a new school. And now there's no Papa Fwelema." He continued to stare at the curb.

"What are you going to do now?"

"I don't know."

"Where are you going to stay?"

"I'll find some place."

"But where?"

Kongolo continued to stare at the curb.

"Then you're coming home with me." Shabami spoke quickly.

"But what will your mama say?"

"My mama will be glad to have you."

"But you don't have any extra room."

"My mama will make room. I know my mama."

Kongolo looked up, for the first time a flicker of hope showing. "Do you really think she will?"

"Of course she will! Come along!"

Shabami's mama did welcome him warmly, and he gratefully settled with them into their one-room, curtain-divided apartment.

He transferred to a night school so he would have time to look for other odd jobs—digging holes, making bricks, anything that would bring in something toward his school fees. The weeks dragged on heavily, the days full from the first sign of dawn when he unloaded fish to the moment he reached home after a six-kilometer walk from evening classes.

He hurried home from another morning at the cold storage, the three fish he had saved from his pay wrapped carefully in a scrap of paper for Shabami's mother.

"Well, Dominique!"

At the sound of a vaguely familiar voice calling his former name, he looked up.

"Dominique! I haven't seen you for ages."

Kongolo recognized a neighbor of the previous year, an elementary teacher who had lived near his sister.

"Is your sister living in this section now?"

"No," Kongolo replied hesitatingly. "I—I had to move again."

"What? More problems with Malela?"

Kongolo nodded.

"Where are you living?"

"With a friend's mother . . . near here."

"And you're still going to school?"

Kongolo named the night school.

"There? And you walk there every night—through that bad section of town?"

"That's the really bad thing," Kongolo replied. "But what else can I do?"

His teacher friend looked thoughtful. "I'll tell you what you can do," he offered. "You can come to live with me."

"With you?" Kongolo asked, surprised.

"I live only a few blocks from that school now—just my brother and me. We have two big rooms—plenty of room for three. Since you study evenings, you could prepare our meals in the afternoon in exchange . . ."

Kongolo did not have to hear the offer a second time. "I'd be glad to!" he exclaimed.

With the move Kongolo was not only nearer his school but also nearer his Catholic church. The weeks rolled into months, and the school year finally neared its close. Exhausted after each long day, he always paused to go through the beads of the rosary before tumbling into bed. "Hail Mary full of grace," he repeated over and over. Mary? he wondered. Can she find favor with God for me? Can she find help for my problems?

"You should come to my church," the teacher invited more than once. "I used to be a Catholic, but I found that the Protestants . . ."

"I'm a baptized Catholic now," Kongolo replied staunchly. "I always wanted to be a Catholic. I will never leave my church."

"It's good to feel sure about your church," the teacher agreed. "As long as you keep your faith, God will honor you. But if you ever want something different . . ."

"Nothing can ever change my mind," Kongolo assured him.

One Thursday when he returned from classes, he felt even more tired, worn out, and discouraged. Days seemed to stretch longer and longer, but the money never added up to what he needed. Another payment was due at school the next week. He wondered how he could have enough money for the payment, if the vicious struggle for an education would ever end. He picked up his rosary and slipped through his prayers. "Will God listen? Will He help in my misery?" he asked himself. When he dropped into bed, he noticed vaguely that the teacher was still on his knees by his bed at his prayers. But exhaustion blurred his eyes, and sleep hung heavily on his body.

"Dominique!"

The sound of his old name again brought Kongolo back to the surface of awareness.

"Dominique!"

Kongolo rolled over, but in the darkness he could not determine the direction of the strange voice.

"Dominique!"

Wide awake now, Kongolo sat bolt upright. "Who's calling me?" he was about to demand.

"I your God have seen you suffering," the voice said. "And I will help you."

Shaken, surprised, Kongolo continued to sit in his bed staring into the darkness. In the faint moonlight that filtered through the curtained window, he could see that the teacher had already gone to bed; he could hear his regular breathing in a sound sleep. "What is the meaning of this?" he asked himself. "I heard a voice calling my name. I heard it. And it said . . . It said . . ." His thoughts troubled him. "It said God has seen me. He will help me."

He lay back down, no longer noticing his tiredness. "God has seen my problems . . ." Gradually sleep again overtook him.

"Did you hear someone calling me during the night?" he asked the teacher in the morning.

"I didn't hear anything."

"Something strange happened," Kongolo continued. "Three times a voice called my old name. And then . . ." He told what he had heard.

"The word of God is sure," his friend replied. "Wait. The answer will come."

All day as he unloaded fish, as he went to his latest job of digging rain-sewer trenches, as he went home to prepare the evening meal, as he went to classes—all that day he waited. But no answer came. The next day, Saturday, he worked in the morning. In the afternoon he went with his friends to confession, then he stayed for the vespers service held in the hour before the sun went down. A younger priest, a new missionary from France, spoke. After the service Kongolo stood outside, visiting with his friends.

The priest came out of the church and stopped on the bottom step. He hesitated a moment as if looking for someone, then he pointed at Kongolo and motioned him to come. "See me in my office after mass tomorrow," he said. "At eleven o'clock."

"Yes, Père," Kongolo replied.

"What's that about?" his friends asked. "Why did he call you?"

"He told me to come to his office tomorrow."

"Why you? Why not the rest of us?"

Kongolo shrugged. "I'll find out tomorrow."

At exactly eleven o'clock the next morning he was knocking on the office door.

"Enter, son," the priest called.

Kongolo opened the door.

"Come in, son, and take a chair." The priest pointed to a chair by the desk. Another boy already sat in the office, and two others were at the door. "You're breathing hard—did you run?"

"Certainly," Kongolo replied. "I looked forward to this."

The priest smiled. "Where do you live?"

Kongolo named the street.

"Do your parents live there?"

"No."

"Who do you stay with, then?"

Kongolo looked at the priest but did not respond directly. "Why do you ask?" he questioned.

The priest turned to the other boys. "You can leave now," he said gently. "We need to talk, son," he continued when the others had gone, closing the door. "If I called you, it is because of a reason. I want to ask you some things. Don't be afraid to answer, even if you don't know why you are here. A strange power pushed me to call you." He looked searchingly at Kongolo. "I find you a likeable young man. Tell me about yourself. To begin, what class are you in?"

"Third-year secondary, commercial section."

"Are you thinking of going into business?"

"I'd prefer to prepare for university entrance . . . into engineering, but—"

"You couldn't get a place in the right school," the priest finished for him. "Who pays?"

"I do. I have contracts and I attend night classes."

"How much do you have to pay?"

"Three zaires a month, and that's not an easy thing."

"Do you have blankets? Mattress? Sheets? Clothes?"

The questions followed each other quickly. "When you first meet someone, you should not say everything," Kongolo thought, reminding himself of the manners his father taught. "Even if you do not have anything that the priest mentions, you must not ask for more than one thing." He began to talk of school. "The thing that weighs very heavy is the money for school."

The priest put his hand into his pocket and pulled out a roll of bills. "Here," he said, handing it to Kongolo. "Pocket money. Pay for your schooling. Buy what you need—blankets, whatever."

Kongolo's mind was reeling. He stammered his thanks.

"You don't have to be bashful with me." The priest spoke kindly. "I know you have your own parents, but from this day I want you to think of me as your adopted father."

Kongolo could hardly believe his ears.

"I want you to leave your night school and come to live with me at the technical prep school where I teach."

"Live with you . . . at the mission?"

The priest nodded and smiled. "Of course you will have to pass the entrance exam, but I'm sure that won't give you any problem. In fact, I want you to come see me tomorrow." He gave the directions. "Remember, come to the priest's residence and ask for Père Stephan."

"Yes, Père—Père Stephan. I'll be there." He felt himself relaxing and beginning to smile. "Père Stephan, how can I ever thank you?"

"It's all right, son." The priest spoke softly. "I am not the one. Direct your thanks to God, our heavenly Father."

13

Time passed quickly. Half day in class, half day in the shop, Kongolo studied with a purpose. On holidays he worked at a city printing press. Shortly before school closed at the end of his fifth year, Père Stephan congratulated him. "You've done very well."

"I've tried my best."

"And I'm pleased to be able to call you my boy." Père Stephan smiled. "I've decided that you should not work at the press this vacation."

"Not work? But next year is my last in secondary. The experience . . ."

"Yes," agreed the priest, "experience is important. And there is no better experience in education than to travel, to see more of the world, to broaden your horizons."

"To travel, Père?"

"Yes, to travel. It is all arranged. When school is out, you will go with me to visit my family. You'll see Paris, my home that I've tried to tell you about. We'll travel the French countryside and in other countries of Europe."

"Paris. Europe." Kongolo could hardly believe what he was hearing. "Oh, Père."

Returning to school after that summer in Europe, he sensed himself a different person. The streets and buildings of Lubumbashi were still impressive, especially when compared with the mud-brick and thatch houses of the villages. But he had seen great castles and grand cathedrals hundreds and hundreds of years old. He had been swept along with the confusing traffic through the streets of Paris—streets bordered with shops and stores and grand department centers filled with riches he had never before dreamed existed.

"What was it like?" his classmates questioned when school began again.

"Wonderful. Beyond description." He shook his head. "The world is full of unbelievable things."

"Is it true that you are going to enter a monastery there, that you are going to study for the priesthood?"

"In order to become a priest, one must be assured that he is called for that work."

"But after living all these years with the priests, surely you will want to become a priest yourself."

"I will always serve my church and honor its teachings. I am very grateful for what the priests have done for me, but the priesthood . . ." As he spoke, he was remembering his father's visit of the week before.

"Remember when I first sent you to Lubumbashi?" his father had asked. "Remember how the people warned me that you would become a bandit? I told them that would never happen. Now do you know what they say?" He did not wait for an answer. "They say that because you live with the priests, you will become a priest. And they say that it would have been better for you to be a bandit." Excitement edged his words. "You are my oldest son. I am the oldest son of my father who was the oldest son of his father. Our children are our pride, they are our future. It would be better if you were dead, they say, than to be a priest who cannot marry and who cannot have children."

"And how do you feel, Papa? Would you be ashamed if I should become a priest?"

"God has been very good to you, my son. He has given you many blessings through this White father who is a priest. Our family is very grateful for what he has done for you, our son. You know that I have always wanted you to study, to learn the ways of this new world, and to follow the way of God. But to become a priest..." His papa sighed deeply. "I am Luba. We Lubas value our children . . . and our children's children."

Kongolo smiled. "I do not feel that God has called me to be a priest," he assured his father. "Père Stephan and I have talked about this. He is sure that God does have something special for my life, but we must wait for that to be revealed."

"And what will you do?"

"I don't know, Papa. After this year I hope to enter the university, but I must wait for God to show me the way."

"That is as it should be," his father agreed. "I, myself, have found now that it is good to go to a church. It is good to worship God with others. You know that the other mama and I have been baptised into the Methodist church."

"Methodist?" Kongolo asked in surprise.

"It seems that is the right way for me—a way that speaks to my heart. Your brothers have found another church. Your own mama goes to the Catholic church, as you do."

Kongolo nodded. "That is good."

"The church will make no difference between you and me," his father continued. "It is right for you to belong to the church of the one who has helped you so much."

That is not the reason, Kongolo wanted to cry out. I love my church. It is the right church. But he remained calm. "I am happy there," is all that he said.

School fell into the usual routine of work and study. With all the talk of his making a good candidate for the priesthood, he began to have questions within himself. Although he was fiercely Catholic , certain things troubled him. "Why do we always pray to the virgin Mary?" he asked one of the priests one evening.

"She is our intercessor with God," the priest replied.

"But why cannot we pray directly to God?"

"Who of us is worthy to approach God directly?" the priest

returned. "The mother of our Lord is highly favored of God, so is it not better that she represent us in heaven?"

"But why, when we pray, must we count these beads? Does that make our prayers better?" Kongolo was serious.

"That is to help us to remember our prayers."

"But can't we pray without . . . ?"

The priest looked at Kongolo directly. "We must be careful of our questions," he warned. "Sometimes thinking too independently can cause confusion."

"Yes, Father," Kongolo replied, lowering his eyes. "Forgive me if sometimes I do not understand."

"Certainly, my son. Just give your mind over to God and to His church. Your people have need of men like you."

"Thank you, Father."

As Kongolo went back to his room, his thoughts tangled about themselves. The priest, he knew, was sincere in his counsel, yet the questions persisted.

"Père Stephan," he asked later, "how is it that many of you priests are so different? You neither drink nor smoke, and you teach me to love honesty. Yet many of your brothers drink in a way that makes the students laugh. They behave in other manners that, well, the students sometimes say that they are more African than we Africans ourselves because they have learned well the ways of cunning and deceit."

"It is sad," replied Père Stephan. "Many of my brothers have studied to be priests, but they have never learned the ways of our Lord. You must not look to man for your example."

Kongolo understood, but still questions haunted him. Then one night in a dream he saw a pretty little town, all of its walks flower-lined. A lone man dressed in a white tunic, with a face brilliantly alive with light, walked about in a garden. In his dream Kongolo approached the man to see better. As he neared, the man spoke. "My name is Jesus Christ." His words flowed in full, round tones. "I am the source of everything, the One who came to this world to give testimony."

As He spoke, Kongolo felt a great happiness sweep over himself. "Lord," he said, "there is one thing that troubles me. I want to know how to pray. How should I pray and of whom should I ask for happiness?"

"My Father and Me," Jesus responded. He came nearer

Kongolo, then continued. "Everything that you are looking for, ask. It is My Father and I who can fill your need. When it is a question of praying, always ask My Father in My name, and your prayer will be answered because I am the light and the life of this world. Above all, do not forget that your God is a jealous God. I am the *only* mediator between God and man."

When he awoke the next morning, the dream remained indelibly on his mind, and he wrote down word for word what he had seen and heard. "If what I have seen is true," he told himself, "then the virgin Mary has no part in our prayers. I wonder . . ." He went to find one of the priests.

"I see," responded the priest when Kongolo had related what he had dreamed. "And you are wondering about this? You are a young man of understanding. Let me tell you honestly that what you have seen is as it is in the Bible."

"What?" Kongolo demanded. "If that is the way of the Bible, then why does the church . . . ?"

The priest raised his hand. "Not so hasty, boy," he warned. "Sometimes the ways of the church do not always agree with the Bible."

"But why?"

"The church has authority from God."

"But what if God reveals to you what is in the Bible and you do not follow it?" Kongolo phrased his question pointedly.

"I am only a priest," replied the man. "I have a job. I do it. I cannot fight the entire church."

Kongolo regarded the older man, a man in whom he had confidence, a man with whom he had often spoken about spiritual things, a man who showed himself a priest from the heart.

"Son," the priest continued, "God has chosen to reveal His ways to you. Guard jealously what He has shown, and He will continue to guide you. He has a special work for you, that I can tell. But there is one thing you must know, one counsel I cannot give you too strongly," He laid his hand on Kongolo's arm. "Always feel free to come to me with your dreams, with your questions. But be careful of talking to others. There are many who would be quick to misunderstand. They will only cause you much trouble."

Kongolo nodded. "I understand," he said quietly.

The priest went to his library. "I want you to have this," he said, taking one of the books from the shelf.

Kongolo took the thick volume. Its title indicated a collection of spiritual readings.

"May God always be with you." The priest's face lighted with a smile. "Before you go, let us pray together and thank God for the wonderful way He has revealed Himself to you."

From that day, in his personal prayers Kongolo addressed God through Jesus, His Son. Outwardly, though, he followed the priest's advice to neither say nor do anything that might upset the spiritual habits of the community. He held the personal revelations to himself, discussing them only with that priest or Père Stephan. At the end of the year he received his secondary diploma, yet unsureness hazed his dream to study civil engineering and to discover to the minutest detail the fascinating world of printing and of presses.

"And now you are ready to go to university?" Père Stephan asked, the day his diploma came.

Kongolo looked earnestly at his adopted father. "If only that could be possible."

"God still sends His miracles," Père Stephan said mysteriously. "I didn't want to tell you this before, because I didn't want anything to hinder you in your preparations for final exams, but . . ." He let his voice trail out a bit. "When I return to Europe next week it won't be for my usual holiday—it is for always. I've been recalled to a parish in Paris."

"Père Stephan! No!" Kongolo burst out. "You can't leave!"

"I must. I have my orders."

"But, Père, what will I do?"

"Kongolo." The priest spoke almost severely. "You have finished your studies at this school, and you have your diploma. You did not think that you could live here indefinitely, did you?"

"No, Père." Kongolo spoke hesitantly. "I have applied to the Lubumbashi University school of engineering, but . . . but . . . I thought you'd still be here. That . . ."

Père Stephan laid his hand on Kongolo's arm. "Sometimes life gives us strange surprises. Remember, son, that first day I called you to my office at the church?"

"How could I ever forget!" Kongolo exclaimed. "I can never begin to tell you how . . . how good it's been to be able to live without the worries of having to keep myself in school. I—I must seem very ungrateful. It's just the surprise. I don't want you to go, but I do want to make you proud of me, to show myself worthy of what you've done for me."

"You've already made me proud of you. You've done well these years. I have confidence that you'll continue to do well wherever God may call you." The priest looked at him searchingly. "Did I ever tell you," he continued, "that when I called you to see me in the office, it was just as much a surprise for me as for you. When I came out of that church, I did not know you. I saw you with those other boys, and it was as if a voice told me, 'Call that boy. Care for him.' I could not stop myself."

"God is great!" Kongolo exclaimed. "The voice in the night—remember the one I told you about?—it was as if God was preparing me for what you were going to do. I always want to serve God, and I want to live up to your confidence in me."

Père Stephan cleared his throat. "There is just one more thing, Kongolo. Do you really want to stay in Lubumbashi and study here in the university?"

"Where else would I go?"

"To Paris."

"Paris?"

Père Stephan nodded, his big smile bursting out again. "It's been difficult to keep all this from you," he admitted, "but I found it best. You will have a scholarship to study in Europe. You can live with my parents. I will leave as planned next week, and you will stay on to get your travel documents in order, then you can come later."

Kongolo shook his head in disbelief. "What can I say? How can I thank you?"

"Direct your thanks to God. He needs you. He is giving you the opportunity."

"God is great!" Kongolo exclaimed again. "I thank Him with all of my heart. And I thank you for letting Him work through you."

14

Kongolo sat at a table in a spacious library, a stack of thick books at his elbow and a huge technical dictionary open in front of him. Pen in hand, blank paper before him, his thoughts strayed far away from the report he had to prepare. He stared out the window to where cement sidewalks blocked off the neatly clipped lawn into tidy squares, where artfully grouped shrubs accented the building contours, and where geometrically bedded flowers added ribbons and rectangles of color, from subdued shades to brilliant splashes. University life more than met his expectations. The only African in his class, he was constantly amazed at the politeness, the courtesy, and the interest his fellow students showed.

"God has certainly blessed these people," he told himself. "The way they think, the way they behave . . . That must be why

God has blessed them so much."

He continued to stare across the campus, but he was no longer seeing its parklike aspect. Instead, in his thoughts, he trudged the hard-packed red-earth street of his home village, scraping the red dust under his plastic sandals. The clumpy tropical grass growing haphazardly down into the open rain sewers accentuated the unevenness of the road lines. The palms waved at irregular intervals—some set back onto family court-yards, some swaying at road's edge—reaching their lofty fronds toward a cloudless sky. The houses, some huddled in family groups, some alone, were all a repetitious mud brown with a sharply sloping, weathered thatch.

In his thoughts he turned into the family parcel and stood looking about the courtyard. A handful of chickens pecked around grass clumps in their endless quest to satisfy their appetites. The grinding bowl, shaped from a stumpy log in the form of a big goblet, lay on its side, the two long pounding sticks dropped beside it under the shade of a palm. The ground around was powdered white from cassava meal that had scattered out when the women did their pounding. Two bamboo chairs sat in the shade of the overhang of the main house.

"An arrow shot into the sky is on a promenade, but the earth is its lodging." The Luba proverb that his father had repeated to him on his visit home for a last goodbye before going to Europe echoed through his thoughts. "That is to say that when someone goes away, it is for the future of his people," his father had explained again.

"Never scorn anything that your neighbor may give you, not even if it is a gift as small as a needle." His mother's last words of advice echoed after those of his father's.

"For the future of everyone . . . Small things . . ." He raised his arms and stretched, flexing his muscles in an attempt to bring his thoughts back to the present. He was one of only a few in the large reading room. He laid his pen down and rested his chin on his hands. "What am I learning here? How will I apply it to the future?"

Lately he had asked himself these questions more and more. "Do I go back and start a printing business in zone headquarters? Do I find investors to develop agricultural projects? Do I stay in Europe to work and use my earnings to help my family back home?" He puzzled over possible answers. With his university studies more than half finished, he needed to seriously consider his options. "Whatever I choose, I do need to go back home, even if only for a visit." He chuckled softly to himself, remembering the counsel of some village elders to his parents.

"Don't let your boy go," they had warned. "You will never see him again. You cannot trust those Whites."

"But what of all the years he has lived with the White missionaries in Lubumbashi?" his father had asked.

"Ah-aaa," warned one wizened old papa. "That is merely a trick. That is here. Now they want to take him away. They will keep him and fatten him in their way, and one day he will be ready for their feast. We know what the White man does to the Black ones he can trick into going away with him."

Kongolo continued to chuckle to himself. "They have fattened me. Not for their feast, but with my feasting on their good food. I wonder . . . will I ever again enjoy cassava pâte and cassava leaves and beans, as I once did?" He stretched again and looked at his watch. "Plenty of time," he told himself. "Christine's not expecting me until . . ."

His thoughts backtracked in another direction. He remembered that winter Sunday of his first year in Paris. He was caught in the squeeze of the crowd leaving morning mass. A heavy, wet snow had fallen during the service. People jammed together at the cathedral doors, waiting to pick their way down the icy stone steps. He paused at the top, ready to take the first step down, when there was a surprised "Oh!" and a sudden thud at his feet. He looked down.

"Pardon me!" he exclaimed, reaching down. "Did I bump you? Here, let me help."

The girl at his feet took his offered hand. As he helped her up, the people flowed to either side, leaving them an island in the mass of humanity. "It wasn't you!" she exclaimed. "This crowd . . . and the ice . . . isn't it dreadful?"

Kongolo nodded. "Let me help you down these steps before anything more happens," he suggested, offering his arm.

"Thank you. You're very kind."

"It's nothing, really," he replied. They reached the sidewalk. "There, now, I hope you reach home without further mishaps." He started to turn to leave.

"Really, you've been very kind." The girl's hand was still on his arm, as if to hold him back. "I appreciate what you've done."

Kongolo smiled. "I could hardly leave you there to be trampled on."

"Not everyone would have done the same. Do you live near here?" she asked suddenly.

"Not far," he replied, naming his street and apartment. Going home, he thought little more of the incident. A week later he was surprised to find the girl at his apartment door. From that time on, he had difficulty getting her out of his thoughts. "But I am a student," he argued with himself. "I am here for studies—and studies only. Besides, what will the others think?" He thought of his family in Africa, and he could already hear their objections.

"What will be her work?" they would ask in their way of questioning that really meant, "Does she have any idea of how an African woman should comport herself?" "Will she eat *sombe* [cassava leaves]?" "Will she carry water from the spring?" they would ask.

He chuckled to himself at the thought of Christine trying to balance a five-gallon pail of water on her head for the half-mile trek back to the village from the spring. He knew that before they became too close as friends, he must face her with the reality.

"Christine," he began one day, "if we become good friends, people will come to you and ask why you go out with a Black, an African."

"But those who follow God don't base their friendships on color," she objected. "They base their friendships on the person, on his manner, on his quality."

"That does not change the fact that I am African," he replied. "I am Black. God created me Black. I am proud to be Black. But not everyone can accept a different skin. There will always be those who disdain my skin." He spoke openly. "I am Black. You are White. I am Luba. You are French. Each of our cultures has its good and its bad. But God has made us as we are, and we must accept ourselves as we are. I find you a very attractive girl, a person of fine qualities, and I do not want a friendship with you that will cause problems."

"I don't care how different our colors are," Christine insisted. "It is the person that counts. Maybe there are some in France who do not accept a person because they do not like his color. But that is mostly an idea of the past. Today the people who are thinking people accept a person for what he is."

"And your parents?" asked Kongolo. "What will they think?"

"If a boy, even if he has black skin, is worthy, they will find no problem."

"You must ask them."

"OK."

"And I will ask Père Stephan and his parents."

"I tell you, there will be no problem."

"First, talk to your parents. Tell me what they say, and then we'll decide." Kongolo remained firm. As soon as he could, he talked to Père Stephan and the priest's father and mother.

"My son, why must you talk about a problem of skin?" Père Stephan's mother demanded. "You're with us and we know you. It is your behavior that counts. There are Africans with White wives here, and their manners are well appreciated. They are educated; they know how to live. It is your friendship. You must decide."

"I want your advice first," Kongolo explained. "I don't want to displease you."

"We as Christians don't consider skin a problem. We see the lifestyle, the manners. Skin . . . Well, when the heart is clean, it is pure, and that is what is important." The woman spoke the sentiments of her husband and her son.

A few days later Christine was back, her long, dark hair framing a face vibrant with happiness. "My parents want to see you!" Excitement underlined her words.

"Now?"

"Yes-yes-yes-yes-yes!" she nearly squealed.

"Our daughter has told us much of what you have discussed," Christine's mother told him. "Her father and I don't know you, but if our girl can't enter into a friendship with you simply because of the color of your skin, then we are no longer Christian, and the apostle Paul condemns us. For us, it is your conduct that counts, not your color. If you are a man worthy, then . . ."

With those words Kongolo felt his worries fall away, and he was happy to be in France, very happy.

He looked at his watch again. "Back to that assignment," he commanded sternly. "If you are a student worthy of the name, you must get this paper finished before you meet Christine."

The months rolled happily toward the end of another school year. With the classes and technical studies he had, he was beginning to feel himself on the way to becoming a qualified printer, designer, and businessman. In order to be thoroughly prepared to establish a business in Africa, though, he must have the technical expertise in repair and maintenance of a press down to the minutest detail. That, he knew, demanded time—years— which he was ready to give. In the end he would have not only a paper confirming a degree in engineering, but he would take home an ability.

In the first week of August he arrived home in Zaire for a visit—his first in more than four years. From the airport it was almost another two days by train to Kitenge. As his train chugged through the countryside he could see that life was changing but he did not notice the progress he had hoped for. At ten-thirty Sunday morning, with the complaint of metal rubbing metal, the train slid to a stop before the Kitenge station.

Climbing down from his compartment, burdened by his heavy baggage, Kongolo searched the faces of those lounging about the platform. He did not recognize anyone. "Do you know where I can find the twins Kyungu and Kabange?" he asked.

The boy he spoke to shrugged his shoulders. "I've heard of them," he replied. "But I don't know where they live. Hey!" he called to some of the others. "Do you know anything about the twins Kyungu and Kabange, where they are?"

There were more shrugs. "I think they live somewhere over there." One of the boys pointed in the general direction of the family home.

The sun beat down, and suddenly Kongolo felt small, very small, and very tired in the oppressive heat. He let his heavy luggage slide to the rough-planked platform, and looked about. The barrier fence from earlier years had fallen into disrepair; small sections of it stood like a few snaggled teeth, while the rest sagged here and there about the ground, giving a derelict atmosphere. He noticed how a road seemed to begin in the middle of a dusty patch then wander crookedly off, as if it had no particular direction to go. The entire scene gave him the feeling that this place had lost its vitality and its interest in making anything of itself. His stomach knotted. "Why did I come?" he wanted to ask himself, feeling very much alone and out of place.

"Would you help me carry my things?" He pointed toward one of the bigger boys, at the same moment pulling some loose change from his pocket.

The boy nodded.

"Dominique!"

Kongolo turned toward the shrill voice calling his old name.

"Dominique! Wako-wako-wako-wako-wako-wako!" The young woman racing toward him seemed a stranger, but her voice gave her away.

"Sister!" he cried, reaching out toward his uncle's daughter.

Grabbing his hands in hers, she began pumping them wildly. "We did not expect you until next train!" she exclaimed. "Come!" In an aside, she spoke rapidly to the boy who waited beside the bags. "Come home, Dominique! Everyone will be so surprised!"

"Home." The word sounded strange. Walking beside this cousin, who chattered quickly on, in the heat, on the dusty road bordered by the patient palms, he began to wonder where his home really was.

"Tutu!" A loud exclamation from the rooftop tore through Kongolo's thoughts. "Tutu!" Kabange slid to the edge of the thatch he had been repairing and jumped down, running. "Wako-wako-wako-wako-wako-wako-wako . . ." Excitement pitching his voice loud and high, he raced toward his big brother and then was pounding on his shoulders with an abandon of happiness.

Caught up in the exuberance of the welcome, Kongolo realized immediately that this sturdy young man was no longer the little boy he remembered. In minutes Kyungu came running from the garden. Soon a large crowd ringed in, everyone shouting and laughing and talking and pounding him on his shoulders until Kongolo wanted to escape the noise and commotion. "Where's Mama?" he demanded.

"In the field."

"And Papa?"

"Out of town. He didn't expect you until next train."

"You've changed. Totally changed." Cousins and uncles and aunts and neighbors pressed closer. "Even the color of your skin has changed. It's lighter."

Kongolo merely smiled. How could he explain the comforts of houses that made people prefer to stay inside rather than always sitting outside? How could he explain the months when the winter sun was weak and often blotted out with snow clouds?

"The way you speak. The way you smile. The way you carry yourself. That has all changed." They clucked their tongues and continued to talk about him as if he were an item of curiosity.

Suddenly a piercing trill, the *mukunda,* the cry of a woman expressing joy, cut through the commotion. Kongolo jumped, then he was hurrying toward his mother. She dropped the hoe she was carrying, wiped her hand on her *pagne,* the wraparound skirt that all the women wear, and reached out to him.

"And you have not yet been washed?" She eyed him with motherly concern. "Hsssssst now," she commanded the others. "Let this boy be. He must wash himself and rest from his long journey. Later you can talk."

With the layers of dust accumulated during the long hours on the train washed away, Kongolo stretched out on his bed. "This is home," he kept repeating to himself. "This is home. Papa wanted me to grow up knowing the two ways, but he always told me I must never forget my home." He stared up through the ceilingless room into the plaited thatch above. "This is my father's house, and I must be proud of it, for this is the way it is."

The cross-country train trek had taken him through village after village, where people had nothing more than bare houses and gardens scratched out of the leached savanna soil. Now he was home . . . home to a house that was a replica of all those he had passed. The stark contrast to his apartment in France forced itself upon him. "The arrow shot into the sky is on a promenade, but the earth is its lodging." His father's proverb came back. "For the future of everyone."

He turned on his side and with his eyes traced the pattern of the mud bricks forming the wall. "With so many needs . . . Where? Where does one start?" His chest knotted with emotion as the realization of the overwhelming lack of progress pressed down. He felt his eyes moisten. He was a man of two worlds. He saw how much the world that was his home needed his learning. And he had no idea of where to begin.

Burying his head in his pillow, he cried shamelessly and helplessly.

15

"What now?" Kongolo asked himself. "I can't let her go on like this. I'm here only a few weeks and it's not fair to my own mama." He sat with his head in his hands on a bamboo stool in front of the house.

"What is it, son?" his father asked, coming out.

"Oh, Papa. It's the other mama," he blurted out, as if he were a little boy again. "She's not happy with the presents I gave her. She says the brothers took what she was to have and gave it to our own mama. She says we do not want her to have anything nice."

"I'll talk to her," promised his father.

Kongolo looked at him reproachfully. "Why the complaints?" he asked quietly. "I didn't come to cause confusion. I'm treating her the same as my own mama, as you have always taught us. Tell her she can come and choose something she likes better." He paused, his thoughts racing back to the letters of the last two years from Kabange and Kyungu.

"Papa has divorced Mama," they had written. "He's making life extremely difficult for us."

Kongolo continued to look at his father. "Why did you do it?" he wanted to ask. But his father had not mentioned the situation. During the entire visit he had been pretending that all was as it always had been. "I want the other mama to be satisfied," he finally said. "I don't want her to cause trouble."

"That is no problem," his father assured him.

"Tell her to come get what she wants," Kongolo insisted. "I don't want her to have any reason to be dissatisfied."

The other mother came later. "I never said anything," she remonstrated.

"Mama," he returned. "Don't be upset. I want you to be happy. Here. I have other things. Choose what you like."

The woman forced a smile. She looked at the blouses and scarves from France that Kongolo had laid out on his bed. "I like that and that," she said at last, pointing.

"They're yours." He pressed them into her hands. "Remember, I am your child too," he said kindly. "What you eat, I eat. The house where you sleep, I sleep. I want you to be happy."

She thanked him and left.

Visitors continued to come. "How do you find Kitenge?" they asked.

"It is my home," he answered truthfully. "But there are habits . . ."

"If we come with many questions," one boy spoke up, "it is because we want to learn. You are our spokesman. We need you to teach us. What are these habits?"

"The African seldom counts on himself," Kongolo replied. "He has the habit of asking for money, for clothes, for things he sees and wants. If it is given, he is never satisfied. If it is refused, he becomes worse."

"When we say we lack something . . ." The boy started to reply, then broke off. "We want to have hope," he said earnestly.

"I understand," replied Kongolo. "But even in our jealousy and in our cunning , which we pride ourselves on, we like to count on our neighbor to accomplish what we are after. But, my brother, in this world, if a man is to make any progress, he must count on himself. Our people have a proverb that says the best fetish is a calabash full of sweat. The idea is there, we just need to learn to practice it."

The boy nodded. "I think I understand."

Later in the afternoon the twins found him in a quiet moment. "Why don't you come to see the church we built?"

He remembered them mentioning their church in a letter. "Maybe later," he hedged. "With all these people, I'm tired."

That night he thought long and seriously about his own future, about Christine, about the possibilities of their coming back to the area together and setting up a printing business, of financing some farm projects. His family held traditional lands out toward his childhood village. He pictured the house he wanted to build—a villa with guest rooms and conveniences, lawns and flowers. He fell asleep, content with the prospect.

Suddenly in a dream he found himself walking a strange road. A vehicle came, and the people on it called him to get aboard. He climbed on, not knowing where he was going. At the next stop an official boarded, checking tickets. Everyone but Kongolo produced a ticket.

"Who authorized you to take this young man?" he demanded angrily of the others.

Everyone began talking at once. "Who? Who? Who?" he insisted, pointing at first one then the other.

A horrible argument broke out.

"You! Get off! Get off!" hollered the official, giving Kongolo a shove.

Kongolo jumped. He began following a river. He still had no idea where he was going, and he wanted to cross to the other side. He walked into the water. Just then a dreadful-looking animal—a dragon with many horns and a red tail, red eyes and a mouth that spewed fire—came up out of the water.

Kongolo stopped in fright, trembling from head to toe. A great crowd of people appeared on the other side, beyond the fierce animal. "Kill him! Kill him!" they shouted. "He must die!"

The animal sprang for Kongolo's head. Its long, pointed claws lashed out at him.

"Kill him! Kill him! Eat him!" the people shrieked again and again.

Kongolo closed his eyes. He stood dead still, not daring to

move, tensing his muscles so he would not tremble. He felt the animal breathing fire at him. "Don't move!" he warned himself. "Don't move or he'll attack!" He remained absolutely still, paralyzed with a horrible fear. He felt the water surge as if the animal were sinking down into it. He opened his eyes a tiny slit and peeked through them. The animal had disappeared. He opened his eyes wider. Moonlight splashed through his window, and he realized he was in his own bed.

A terrible trembling seized him as if he were still in the grip of the terror of his nightmare. "What does this mean?" he demanded of himself. He could not shake the fear, the sense that something dreadful was about to happen. "What is wrong?" Answers would not come. Still trembling, he slipped from his bed and knelt beside it. "God," he prayed, "take this terrible fear from me. Give me Your peace."

When he lay down again, fear continued to grip his thoughts. "I've never seen such things. What is it that is not going well?" He thought of the long-ago night when he had heard the voice calling his name. He thought of how Père Stephan had called him two days later and of the happy years since. He thought of the dream of Jesus explaining how to pray. Morning came at last, and the day passed without incident. Early the following morning, a Saturday, he got up and went outside. The day seemed unusually hazy. Looking up into the sky, he stopped short, startled. He blinked his eyes and looked again. It was as if he were looking into a cloud of smoke. Wherever he looked the cloud was there. If he covered his right eye, the cloud disappeared. "It must be something from my sleep," he told himself.

He rubbed the eye. He opened and closed it many times. He washed it. Nothing made any difference. The fear he had felt the previous night began to grip him again. "What's wrong?" he worried. "What's wrong with my eye?"

The day dragged by. No change. He did not want to tell anyone about it. The next morning when he got up, smokey clouds filled both eyes. He did not know what to do.

"Dominique!" his Uncle Sondashi called. "Dominique, are you coming to mass with me this morning?"

Kongolo went out. "I can't, Papa Sondashi!" he exclaimed. "Something has happened to my eyes." The fear still weighted him as he explained the problem to his uncle. "Papa Sondashi, am I losing my eyes?" he demanded. "Without my eyes, what will happen to my studies?"

"God is just," was all his uncle could say.

"Without eyes I will not be needed by the African world. What will I do? Return to Europe?"

His uncle shook his head. "I am going to church. I will pray for you to find an answer."

Kongolo went back to his room. "What's wrong? What's wrong?" he demanded, falling on his knees. "What if I lose my eyes? Oh, God, You create. You can solve my problems. Understand me, God. Please understand. Man does not study to have nothing. Man does not plant to not harvest. Understand the misery of my people." Finally he got up and went out.

"What's wrong, Tutu?" Kabange looked at him strangely.

"My eyes," Kongolo replied, and told him the story.

"Tutu! That's impossible!" Kabange exclaimed. "Nothing can happen to you now."

"We'll see." Kongolo's voice held little hope. "Is there a hospital or a dispensary in town?"

"A dispensary."

At the dispensary the nurse talked of certain parasites. "I've treated many cases," he said reassuringly. "Come twice a day, and I will put medicine in your eyes. Take some vitamins, too. With all the traveling and change in diet, it is likely you need them."

Kongolo left the dispensary, hopeful. But as the week continued there was absolutely no improvement in either eye.

"This is strange," the nurse declared. "I've treated many, many cases. They all begin to clear up immediately. As soon as you are back in France, you should see a doctor."

"We see this sickness is very serious," the people began to say to him as word got around. "We pity you, and we are going to give you some advice. We don't want your studies to be for nothing. We don't want you to lose your life."

"God has given me the opportunity to study," he replied. "If God sees it good that I be cured, He will arrange that, too."

"God? Who is this God?" they demanded. "We know only the traditional doctors who can make strong fetishes."

"God is stronger than any fetish or any medicine man," Kongolo replied stoutly.

"Don't you see that it is finished for the big one." The people began talking to the twins. They opened their eyes wide while talking. The belief that when a part of the body is touched mysteriously then it must be regarded as an ominous sign pushed them to urge their cure. "You can't leave him like this. Don't let him talk of his God. In his problem, you must search for other help. Make an effort for him."

At the word "effort" Kyungu and Kabange shook their heads. "We believe in God," Kyungu affirmed. "We believe that God will cure our brother when He finds it good."

People continued to come with their discouraging counsel. "You came back, and look what has happened. Look at the spell that has been cast on you!" one exclaimed. "Me, if I had a chance to go to Europe, I would never come back."

"Is that the way you comfort the sick?" demanded Kongolo. "By coming with shocking words? You should be asking me why I am here. If God wants me to lead a miserable life, I will. I will neither be the first nor the last. In Europe the fashion is to think. If I have gone there to learn, it is to bring back knowledge. And you ask me why I have come."

"Then why don't you make an effort to be healed?"

"I am a Christian."

"Other Christians go to fetishers."

"This is the work of God," Kyungu spoke up. "Our brother will not go to the fetisher. If you read the Word of God, you will see that He created all, even the fetisher. Before God, nothing is difficult. We have faith."

When the time came for Kongolo to return to France, the condition had not improved. The custom was that on the night before a child was to travel, the important members of the family gathered in counsel. His mother, his father, his paternal uncle, and the twins sat with him in the main room of his father's house.

His mother spoke first. "It is better that you return quickly to France to find help for your eyes. You are a treasure for us. We, your parents, have hardly done anything for you. It is those others, those people from a different world, who have helped you. The influence of God has worked. We don't want you to lose the good manner you have gained. Go back. Continue your studies. Advance in this life."

As she spoke Kongolo realized the great appreciation she had for what the White man had done for the African.

"Imagine what God has done for us," she continued. "To take a child, to support him, is no small thing." She looked upward. "God is good," she exclaimed. "Even if you suffer, we know that you will find your life again. Those who have helped you have done it to help our part of the world. God Himself will guide. He will protect you."

Then his father spoke. "Certainly, son, your mother's words are true. A divine force, not human, has worked. That man has supported you. It comforts me that the world has people who love others. One can never believe all the surprises God has. I have not given you anything.

"Now you have come. You have fallen sick. God only knows how you will be cured. They may talk of traditional things, of making an effort. I know you understand. We have always taught you that the ways of evil and the ways of light cannot be mixed. Only God will protect you. No matter where you go, God will be with you. We want you to be a light.

"We wish you bon voyage. We will stay as you have found us. And we hope that with the love of God you will be back."

The words "We will stay as you have found us" touched Kongolo deeply. Yet he said nothing immediately. He waited until his father finished speaking. Then it was his turn to reply. "Being a child," he began, "I have some notions that may also be necessary for you." He looked toward his father. "As is the old custom, you, not having any son, took our mother as your second wife after her husband, a person of your family, died. You fathered us. We grew. You wanted us to study. We studied. You wanted us to be faithful in our work. We have worked hard at all we have found to do. You wanted us to be good examples. We have tried to abide by the good manner you have taught us. If we had grown up as barbarians, I could not have gone abroad to study. To arrive where I have been shows something—it shows parents who have taught us well."

Kongolo paused and looked at the floor. Sadness and hurt welled within him. He remembered the twins' letters. "You say that you will stay as I have found you," he began again. "While I have been here, you have tried to act as if all is well." Kongolo shook his head. "But the discord and the tension are here. You, our example, how could you divorce our mother? How could you, without warning, send her from your care as you did? Instead of maintaining the peace that you taught, you created problems.

"If it were not for our uncle here, my mother would have had nowhere to go. He gave a place to build, and the twins have made her a new house. If it were not for my uncle, my brothers would not have been able to continue their schooling." The twins' description of how suddenly one day, incensed by the jealous complaining of his first wife, his father had ordered his mother and the twins from his house tore at his thoughts. He bit back further words he wished to say.

"We've always counted on you and esteemed you," he continued calmly. "The blessing of God on a family is not a simple matter. If you consider us a gift of God, you must also respect us. You have repudiated Mama, my mother. If you have confidence in me, you should not have caused me shame. The manner of this divorce does not give us any pride. But you have done it. The two of you are here now because, even in divorce, this is the manner of our people. What is done is done. I am your child. I ask that you avoid further problems and discord and conflict. Live in harmony and this will be considered by those around. You represent the face of God here. Continue in the light—the light of the way of that dream you had long ago. Let us have the joy to know that we have parents worthy of the name.

"I have come to visit. I have fallen sick. I can no longer see to read and to write as I should. I do not know the problem, but God does. I am returning to France now, and I have faith that I will be healed. Praise God for His goodness. Let us pray together before I leave."

The six of them knelt on the hardened-earth floor in the shadowy light cast by the small kerosene lantern. Kongolo prayed for protection and for peace in the family.

The night was moonless and darkness hung heavy. The twins collected his things to carry to the station. Then, by the light of the lantern, the small group made their way down the road to await the night train.

16

"Kongolo! Kongolo!"

As he strode out of customs and into the big, bright waiting room of the Charles de Gaulle Airport, Kongolo thrilled to hear the voice he had missed so much. Putting down his bags, he held out his arms.

Christine came rushing toward him. "Kongolo!" she exclaimed again. She stopped short. "What is it?" she asked quickly. "What's happened?"

He dropped his eyes. Relief and sadness surged together. "I don't know," he said huskily. "I just don't know."

"You're so thin!" Concern flooded Christine's voice. "You don't look well." She flung her arms about him. "What is it?" she demanded again.

Conflicting feelings raged through Kongolo. Happiness at

being with Christine. Torment because of his eyes. "Something has happened with my eyes. I . . . Oh, it's good to be with you again." He kissed her gently and held her close. "Where's your car? I want to go home. We can talk on the way."

The next morning he went to a doctor for a thorough examination, but with no results. He was referred to a specialist. The weeks blurred in a round of consultations, examinations, and experiments with different medicines. Still his eyes did not improve. If anything, they became worse. He tried to read, to study. The gritty gray haze in his eyes blurred everything, as if someone had spilled ink across the pages and all the words ran together.

"You can't go to school like this," Père Stephan sympathized. "Better you stay home until we solve your problem. I'll make arrangements with the university."

Kongolo visited more doctors. He saw yet another specialist. The doctor shook his head. "I don't know of anything that will help your condition," he said kindly. "The best advice I can give is for you to go home, to wait and see if there is any change."

"Wait?" demanded Kongolo. "How long will this take?"

"I don't know," the doctor admitted frankly. "You have a condition that we do not understand."

"Is there anyone anywhere who can help?"

"I don't know," the doctor replied again.

"Is there any hope?"

The doctor drew a long breath. "I cannot really tell you. The condition is rare. We have no treatment. There is a possibility the eyes may change of themselves. Other than that, all I can tell you is to wait. I'm sorry."

The way the doctor spoke, Kongolo understood that the hope was small, infinitely small. He returned to the apartment feeling defeated, totally unsure of what to do next. He slumped into his chair. "God," he demanded, "what am I to do? Without my eyes, what good are my studies? My life is consecrated to You. You inspired Père Stephan to support me in my studies. I planned to go back to my people to share what I have learned. And now, what? Am I to suffer? Is it Your plan that I suffer for You? If so, give me the courage. Give me that courage!"

He was still sitting in his chair when Père Stephan came in much later. "What is it, Kongolo?" he asked gently.

"My eyes." Kongolo drew a deep breath. "The specialist says

he can do nothing. He tells me to wait. To wait! Perhaps there will be some change. Perhaps! Père Stephan, already I have been waiting three months. Three months! And I have been able to do nothing. How much longer will this continue?" He spread his hands and shook his head.

Père Stephan continued to listen quietly.

"I see that the only thing for me to do is go back to Zaire and wait there. I cannot continue here as I am."

"But you can stay," Père Stephan interrupted. "You can stay here as long as you need."

Kongolo shook his head. "After all you have done for me? Stay here and be a burden? No. No!"

"You are no burden, son. You are always at home in our house."

"I appreciate what you are saying, Père. And I can never thank you enough—for everything. You have been more than a father. Your parents have truly given me a home. But I know within myself that I must go back to Africa. Maybe there I will be healed. Maybe God has a reason for me to go."

"And Christine? Have you talked with her about this?"

Kongolo shook his head slowly. "I wanted to talk with you first. I need your help with arrangements—I think I should leave just as quickly as possible. I'll tell her tonight, but it won't be easy,"

Père Stephan smiled understandingly. "No. It will not be easy for either of you." He laid a hand on Kongolo's shoulder. "But our Lord will give you courage," he said. "He cares. He will guide. He has a plan for your life, a plan obscure at this moment, but He will not forsake you, of that I am sure."

Kongolo soon had his tickets. Père Stephan's and Christine's families accompanied him to the airport. The others wished him bon voyage, then he and Christine were alone.

"Kongolo, I'm coming with you."

"You're what?"

"My parents and I think it is better."

"But . . . You can't!"

"Wait until the next flight. I can get my ticket."

"But . . ." He looked down at the slender girl, eyes brimming. He thought of the long flight, the days on a boat, then more days waiting for a train. He thought of the thatched, mud-brick, dirt-floored house with no water, no electricity, no conveniences.

He thought of the family who had no idea he was coming. His heart ached to say, "Yes. Yes, come." But he knew he could not. He shook his head firmly.

"You're sick. Will you be all right? You will get home, won't you? You will not do . . ." Her voice caught. "You will not do anything to yourself."

Kongolo took her hands in his. Through the mist that clogged his eyes, even hazier now with tears that wanted to come, he could still see the familiar form before him. "Don't allow yourself such thoughts," he warned. "It is God who gives life. I could never do anything against Him."

"Will . . . will you be all right?"

"I will be all right." He forced himself to speak confidently. "I must go alone this time. Your life is here, your studies. Besides, we'll write. Oh, Christine, I'll be looking for your letters, even if it takes me all week to make out the words." He forced a smile.

"We'll write," she echoed huskily.

Impulsively, he drew her close. "God has many miracles." He spoke with assurance now. "The university has given me two years. Your parents have also given us that time. When I'm back, we'll set the date for our wedding."

"Oh, Kongolo, I don't want you to go."

"It is not an easy thing." Even as he spoke, the loudspeaker announced his flight. He bent to kiss her. "I must go." He picked up his carryon and looped its strap over his shoulder. "God is great!" he exclaimed, trying to force enthusiasm into his voice. "If it is His will, I will be back. I will be back!"

Walking toward the boarding gate, he felt himself being stripped of the way of life he had grown to love in this country that had taken him in. His entire being revolted at the sense of injustice he felt. Kongolo found his place and sank dejectedly into the seat. The big jet engines roared to life, and the plane taxied toward the runway. He leaned his head against the window. The jet gathered its forces and hurtled itself skyward. Through the haze and the tears in his eyes, he looked down at Paris—Paris, home of his unfulfilled dreams. In the distance stood the Eiffel Tower.

The tower. His thoughts tormented him. Symbol of this great industrial world. Symbol of all I am leaving behind. The tower shrank quickly, and a misty gray swathed the plane, blotting France from his view. And his tears rolled down unchecked.

17

Kongolo slumped on a bamboo stool in the shade of the thatch on his father's house, his head propped against his left hand. A crowd pressed close—family, neighbors, the curious, the onlookers. Questions flew. "Why did you come?" "When?" "It disturbs us to see you back so soon." "What's wrong?" "Can't you explain it to us?"

Even as they were posing their questions, he could sense the whispers growing. "This is the end. He has returned to die."

"The problem that brings me here is my sickness." He spoke weakly, sadly. "Otherwise, I would not have come. My eyes are stopped. I can no longer see as I should."

"We find your case very touching." One of the village notables, passing by on an errand for the chief, had stopped and pushed his way through the crowd. He stood before Kongolo, his concerned face shaded by the droopy brim of his plumed hat. The leopard skin tucked apronlike over the long white wraparound covering his street clothes showed his rank in the chief's family. "We need to make an effort with you."

"There's a doctor 'en bois,' a medicine man who works with roots," one of the neighbors interjected. "He is known to make cures for even the strongest evil spirits."

Kongolo listened patiently. "I follow what you are saying," he responded listlessly. "But for the moment I have no such thoughts. This is a case that God Himself will solve."

"This is a case that must be treated as it should," the notable argued. "When one is touched in such a manner, one must search out the cause and then the appropriate cures."

Hours passed. Still people drifted into the courtyard to see this one who had studied so brilliantly in Europe and in whom the light had now gone out. Tired though he was from the days and days of travel, Kongolo continued to repeat his story. That night the family gathered in council to discuss his serious situation. "The only solution we can find is to confide this problem to God," they concluded at last. "Whatever happens, we do not want you to listen to any of this talk about traditional cures."

"I know that has never been the way of our family," he agreed. "My problem rests in the hands of God."

"It is not for nothing that we have given you such strong counsel," his father explained later when they were alone. "When you were in France, in this very house where we are sitting, in the very room where you are sleeping, we experienced the protection of God against the powers of darkness. As you may know, a boy from one of the sisters of your mother's family came to stay with us so he could attend school. Of course we made him welcome. He was something of a troublemaker, but we thought little of it.

"One afternoon a sudden thunderstorm blew up. The boys took refuge in the house. I was out in the kitchen with your other mother. Suddenly we heard a terrible explosion, and I saw smoke billow up through the thatch of the house. Fear grabbed at me. I was certain the boys were finished. But in the next moment they rushed out of the house—all of them."

"God is great!" Kongolo exclaimed.

"God is indeed great!" his father echoed. "When the storm passed, the neighbors came from all sides, shaking their heads with wonder, demanding to know how it was possible that no one was even hurt, exclaiming that our family must indeed have exceptional protection against such forces. After the crowd had gone their ways, the boy came to me. 'A strong power has protected this house,' he said, looking at me strangely.

" 'The God of heaven has kept us from harm,' I replied.

"The boy seemed very troubled. 'I must show you something,' he explained. He took me into the twins' room, the room you have now, and began to dig into the floor. Soon he uncovered some strange objects—the center section of a human skull, fragments of bone, other charms. Immediately I understood. 'What is it you wish to tell me?' I asked.

"By now he looked very frightened. 'If lightning is called down and it does not touch the one intended—it will not rest until it gets someone.'

" 'And whom did you intend that it strike?' I asked.

"He avoided my eyes. 'I paid the sorcerer to strike Kyungu.' "

"Kyungu?" broke in Kongolo. "But why Kyungu?"

"The boy had borrowed money from Kyungu. Later, when he had money, he refused to pay. Kyungu insisted. Rather than pay . . ."

"But I thought the 'lancer de foudre' must warn his victim in advance."

"In the case of thieves—in order to get back that which is stolen. Otherwise, no. An enemy does not announce his intentions."

"And the boy?" Kongolo asked.

"He gathered up his things, without us even asking, and went home. His father came later, trying to appease us. He also is a sorcerer, one with powers strong enough that he dares to openly practice his ways."

"But the boy and the lightning?"

"He is still with his family. He must have made his arrangements with the sorcerer. You know, son, with all the education that has come to our country, these ways of our ancestors are still very much with us, as they were when we first moved back to the village when you were little. Some things are open, some secret. The counsel I gave you then is just as necessary now. Avoid any possible complications. Never eat or talk or go with those you do not know."

"I understand, Papa," Kongolo replied, remembering the story of the boy who had been tricked with the pineapples.

"People will continue to try to convince you. Our people do not reason in the same manner as you have learned. For any sickness, for example, they will not think, Oh, I have a stomachache. I must have eaten something that was not good. No! Immediately they will think, Ah. I must go to the sorcerer to see who it is that is causing me trouble. And the sorcerer will name someone, family or stranger, living or dead, that must be appeased. Son, don't listen to them."

"No, Papa."

"They will come to you saying that you must pay the sorcerer to find who has stopped your eyes, and only then can you be cured. Don't listen."

"Papa, don't worry!" Kongolo exclaimed. "You have always taught us to follow the way of light, to put our trust in God. After all God has done for me, even if I am suffering, do you think I could go against Him?"

"It is good to have such sons as you," replied his father. "You, your younger brothers. People have come to me saying they wished their sons were as reliable, as trustworthy."

"You have taught us well, Papa."

"Your younger brothers are very much given to the ways of God. This little church they are involved with, the one some teacher urged them to attend some years ago, no doubt they have told you about it."

"They mentioned things in their letters—you mean the church they built?"

"That one." His father smiled. "It seriously occupies their time. They teach and they preach. I'm glad for their faith, but I have not seen the great importance they find in that little church."

"Do you still go to the Methodists?"

His father nodded.

"Papa. There's something that still bothers me." Kongolo tested his words carefully before speaking. "The twins—they say there is peace in the family now, that you treat them and mama with respect. But . . . Papa, why the divorce?"

His father seemed to study the skin rug stretched in front of his bamboo chair. "It is not an easy matter to live with two women," he said at last. "Every day one must live with the complaints of the one about the other. And the other about the first. And one must treat both of them the same. And love them the same?" He shook his head sadly. "When our ancestors left us the ways of polygamy, they did not give us an easy thing."

"But . . . why Mama?"

"Polygamy is not an easy thing" was all his father would say.

Each morning Kongolo awoke to find the same grainy haze blocking his vision. "An arrow shot into the sky is on a promenade," he thought miserably, "but the earth is its lodging." He shook his head sadly. "This arrow has returned to its home broken—an arrow that may never reach its mark," he said to himself. No one could offer him any concrete hope.

"Why don't you come to our church?" Kabange and Kyungu urged. "You and Mama. Just to visit."

"One week," Kongolo promised offhandedly.

"Why not this Saturday?"

"Well . . ." He tried to think of an excuse, but, after all, sitting at home or sitting at church would make little difference. "Oh, all right," he agreed reluctantly.

That Saturday morning Kongolo was one of six persons attending services in the little bamboo Seventh-day Adventist church on the edge of town. Kyungu preached. As he spoke about how to grow in faith, Kongolo found himself listening with rapt attention. "Where has this little brother learned to preach like this?" he asked himself in astonishment, remembering the little boy who had carried the machete on their trapping expeditions. "How has he learned this fashion of explaining the Bible, never having studied theology?"

Afterwards, he posed the same question to the twins.

"We traveled to find a preacher to teach us," they explained matter-of-factly. "We asked how to preach. We asked for passages to study. We have studied—and we take turns preaching."

Amazing, thought Kongolo. In the following weeks the boys had little trouble convincing him to come with them to church. He also faithfully continued to attend Sunday morning mass.

Letters came regularly from Christine. With each one's arrival he would shut himself into his room and pore over the pages, trying to separate the words on the paper from the blotches in his eyes. Read a little. Rest. Read a little. Rest. He would not entrust what she had to say to the coldness of some stranger to read to him. Physically his body revolted at the inactivity he felt forced into. An avid gymnast in France, he had lost all interest in exercise. Home about five months, he was attacked with a heavy fever. He lay in bed, weak, nauseated, day after day. His muscles ached. The joints in his back were wracked with pain. He burned with fever. He shook with chills. And his eyes. He could never escape the imprisoning haze that filled them.

"Let me die!" he screamed out to God. "Let me die!" He tore at his blankets. "Let me escape this horrible suffering!" He forced himself from bed. Drawing on his clothes, he walked shakily to the door. "I've got to get away!" His mind worked feverishly, erratically. "I can't take it any longer. My eyes! My body! Oh, God . . . Where are You?" He staggered into the street.

"Tutu! Tutu!" Kabange suddenly appeared before him. "Where are you going?"

"I can't stand this any longer!" Kongolo nearly screamed.

"Tutu. Come." Kabange took his arm. "Come with me." He spoke soothingly. "A visitor is coming—Pastor Mutombo from Kabongo. We are just going to the station to meet him. Wait in the house until he comes. The Papa is not here, so wait to greet him as our elder brother."

Kongolo calmed and let himself be led back into his room. He lay down, but his body ached, and he felt hot, too hot. He drifted into a doze.

"Wafwako, mukelenge!" ("Thank you, important friend.")

A cheery voice seemed to fill the room pronouncing the greeting of warm respect used for someone who is admired to the point one cannot dare to say his name. Kongolo looked up through the haze. A stranger smiled down at him. *"Wafwako, mukelenge,"* he repeated, taking Kongolo's hand. "I am sorry to hear of your illness. But God is good, and He will hear your prayers."

In spite of his misery, Kongolo felt himself wanting to smile at this vibrant personality.

"I've come to spend some time with your brothers at their church," the pastor explained. "We'll have meetings each day, but *mukelenge,* I don't want to preach if you can't come."

"I'll come if I am able," Kongolo heard himself replying weakly.

"And we'll pray that you will be able," the pastor responded.

"Let's pray now."

By the day the meetings began, Kongolo was up and about. Attracted by Pastor Mutombo's vibrancy and his convincing explanations of the Bible, he attended each of the meetings. At the end of the series, the pastor asked for those to stay who wanted to practice what they had been studying.

"You can put my name down," Kongolo volunteered.

"Would you like to be baptized?" the pastor asked.

"Baptized!" Kongolo exclaimed. "I'm already baptized."

"But there is another baptism."

"If I say I am going to continue to come to this church, it is only because I wish to have more knowledge of the doctrines of the Bible. I wish to enrich my belief. I do not ever intend to change my religion."

Daily Kongolo's thoughts went back to Europe. He wrote Père Stephan and Christine about the biblical discoveries he was making. Both wrote back to encourage him. He found the old sewing machine that his father had saved from before the revolution. Since he had learned to sew in France, and as he could still see well enough to work with the machine, he soon developed a clientele for a small tailoring business. A year had passed since he had left Europe.

One night in a dream, a brilliant light shown before him. As he looked along the light, in the distance he saw Jesus in the River Jordan being baptized. "The baptism of Jesus?" he asked himself when he awoke. "A light leading to the baptism of Jesus. What does this mean? What is the significance of the baptism of Jesus for me?"

Another dream the following week left him even more puzzled. As he was sleeping a person approached him. "Has White welcomed you?" he asked.

Startled by the sudden appearance of this person and the mention of the strange-sounding name, he replied, "No!"

The man disappeared.

The following night he dreamed exactly the same dream. The third night he again saw the same man coming toward him. "Has White welcomed you?" he asked again.

"No!" Kongolo replied.

"White?" he asked himself the next morning. "White?" The word felt strange on his tongue. It had no sense of French or of any word from any of the African languages he spoke. "White? Three times the question about this person named White. What is the meaning of it?" He went to see his friend, the Catholic lay pastor. "Have you ever heard of a person named White?" he asked.

The pastor shook his head.

He asked others. No one could give him any idea about the name. "White?" he puzzled. "The dream of Jesus' baptism." He began to feel uneasy, restless, as if somehow those dreams might push him toward a decision he did not want to make. "If I find this name in any church, I will have to consider it a call. One I cannot refuse," he warned himself.

A few days later, to his surprise, he saw Pastor Mutombo coming up the road toward his house. "Pastor!" he exclaimed, hurrying to greet him. "What brings you to Kitenge?"

"I've come to see how the church and you are doing. I wanted to come sooner, but . . ." He looked at Kongolo piercingly. "How are you doing, *mukelenge?*"

The genuine interest in the pastor's voice cut right to the trouble in Kongolo's heart. "Pastor," he asked impulsively, "do you know any significance for the name White?" He told Pastor Mutombo of the dreams.

"Oh, la-la!" exclaimed the pastor. "Oh, la-la! What an honor for my life! What a recompense for my work! White! White!"

Kongolo watched the pastor's reaction with bewildered amazement.

"White!" exclaimed the pastor again. "She is a prophet of the Adventist Church."

"The Adventist Church!" Kongolo repeated. Suddenly the impact of the meaning of what he was hearing swept over him. "The Adventist Church," he repeated weakly. "Then this is a call I cannot refuse."

Kongolo talked long and earnestly with the pastor that day. "What can I do to be baptized?" he finally asked.

18

Kongolo sat at his table, trying to fit the events of the past weeks into words that could carry the comprehension of what he had discovered. "Christine will understand," he reassured himself as he struggled to make his pen keep the words flowing across the page without becoming confused with the flakey haze that screened his eyes. He sat, attention lost to the afternoon, totally given to the thoughts of what he was sharing.

"Good afternoon, son."

Startled by the deep voice, a voice that carried the unmistakable tone of the priesthood, Kongolo jumped back to reality. "Good afternoon," he replied, turning toward the open door. He hurried to welcome the stranger, a European. "What good wind has brought you here?" he asked, inviting him in and showing him to a place on the bamboo settee beside his table.

Sitting down, the priest looked at Kongolo as if making an assessment. Then he began to nod his head.

"Why are you nodding?" Kongolo finally asked.

"I did that in a sense that means a lot," the priest replied. "Because you are a child of hope, we count on you. Don't think that we forget the names of any of you who leave for Europe. On coming into town the other day, I heard what you're starting to do, and what I've heard is not good."

Kongolo listened silently to the priest, the curé of a distant mission.

"What has pushed you to join with this little church? What is it that you have missed with us? Don't you eat or sleep as you should? Have you been badly treated?"

Kongolo shook his head. "No. No. It is not that at all!" he exclaimed. "I have not been mistreated. It . . . it is the light I have found," he continued, searching for words to explain himself.

"Light? What light?"

"The light that one calls the Word of God," Kongolo answered simply. Then he posed a question of his own. "And how does one discover this light of the true church?"

"The commandments," the priest answered briefly.

"Then let's follow them," Kongolo suggested.

The hours of the afternoon slipped away in serious discussion. "I understand what we have discussed," the priest said at last. "The problem I find, though, is that I am not at all satisfied with the fact that you have left the church. It can be seen as though you have rejected all that has been done for you."

"Becoming a Seventh-day Adventist does not say that I look badly upon the Catholic Church. My father and I have discussed this decision. Although neither Catholic nor Adventist, he has always been a man of understanding. He seriously cautioned me to first write Père Stephan, my adopted father. He told me that if the Père accepts, then he thinks there should be little difficulty with the others. I have written Père Stephan and he understands. He sees that I must follow the light that has been revealed to me; for how can I defend myself if I go against what God has revealed? How can I defend myself if I do not act according to what the Bible says?"

"I see," the priest said thoughtfully. "You are a brave young man. Keep up your courage. Be courageous." He stood to leave.

When the two of them went out of the house, the sun nearly touched the horizon, casting long shadows of the buildings and the palms toward the road. "Do you know why I say to be courageous?" the priest asked. "There will be events. There will be surprises. Be firm. Even when I heard talk of you, I sensed this was a firm decision you had taken and I knew I must come to talk with you, for this is a decision that not everyone will understand."

When the priest was gone, Kongolo pondered what he had said. "Why would anyone want to create problems for me?" he asked himself. The question soon faded with his preparation to travel to Songa, the nearest Adventist mission, about 150 miles (250 kilometers) away. "There are missionaries, teachers, and pastors who can study with you," Pastor Mutombo had told him. "Besides, *mukelenge,* the missionary doctor there may have some answers about your eyes."

"And when you come back, we'll go to your church together to see how the preaching there is different from that at my church," his father promised.

Arriving at Songa, he studied the Bible daily with one or another of the mission staff, asking questions, clarifying doctrine. He also went to see the doctor. "There's nothing I can do," the doctor told him matter-of-factly, after hearing his story. "I've heard of a few cases like yours. A deterioration releases small particles that float across the field of vision. I know of no cure."

The doctor's words dropped like cold stones onto Kongolo's hopes. "Isn't there anything anyone can do?" he demanded, grasping for at least some word of encouragement.

The doctor shook his head. "Nothing I've heard of," he replied. "But," he added, as if holding out a possibility, "with the advances in nuclear medicine, there might be a new discovery—perhaps in America or Europe."

America, Kongolo thought dejectedly. How could I ever get to America? Europe? I've already seen more than my share of doctors and specialists there. He drew a deep breath. "Thank you, doctor," he said quietly.

Back in the mission guest room, he struggled with this new bad news. With his visions of White and of Jesus' baptism and his decision to come to Songa to study for his own baptism, he had felt a hope that God was leading him to a means of cure. Now that hope, too, was gone. "God is my only hope," he told himself. "My *only* hope!"

He fell to his knees by his bed. "God!" he prayed. "I have followed what You have shown me. I have given my life completely and totally to You. I have dedicated myself to Your service. But, God, my eyes. My eyes! Hear me! Heal my eyes!"

The hours wore long into the night. Still he pleaded with the Lord. At last he crawled into bed, exhausted, and fell into a deep sleep. In the morning he got up and sat at the table with his Bible before him. As he sat there, forcing his eyes to focus on a short passage of Scripture, he felt something like a large, round tear roll from each of his eyes. They dropped to his Bible.

What? he exclaimed within himself, picking them up. Little globes filled with what looks like red and yellow and white threads. A strange sensation passed over him. "Is this Your answer, God?" he suddenly asked aloud, looking heavenward. "Are You unstopping my eyes?" Excitement grabbed at him. He looked down at his Bible. The print did seem somewhat clearer. But the band of haze remained, and soon the words, as always, began to blur together.

Setting his Bible aside, he began to pray again. "I do not understand what has happened," he explained. "And I still do not see as I should." He prayed through the day and into the night. The next morning two more of the thread-filled drops rolled from his eyes. Again his vision seemed to clear. The next day was Sabbath. He got up and prepared himself for church. In the afternoon everyone gathered at the place where the river that rushed past the mission eddied into a quiet pool. Just as he had seen Jesus do in his vision, he walked down into a river and was baptized. The next morning he stopped by the mission director's house.

"How is it today?" the director's wife asked when she came to the door.

Kongolo smiled. He felt as if he were about to burst with happiness. "Good!" he exclaimed. "Very good! Yesterday was the happiest day of my life. I am a new person. Now the only joy for me is to work for my God." He paused and then looked at her questioningly. Standing on the brown stone walk, his slender form erect to its full five-foot-seven, he felt a confidence surging through his person. Yet he was compelled to ask the question. "What does it mean," he began, "when a person is standing in a circle of light and light is coming in toward him and going out from him?"

The director's wife hesitated before answering. "Did you have another dream?"

He nodded. "Yes. This morning."

"And who was the person?" Her smile told him she already knew the answer.

"That is the question," he responded.

"Search," she replied. "You will find the answer." Then she added, "Kongolo, God has a work for you. An important work."

When he was back in his room, the words continued to ring in his ears. "Search. God has a work for you." At the time, he told no one about his prayers or his eyes, but he kept careful notes in his journal. Throughout the week he pleaded with God. Each morning another multicolored globule rolled from each eye, some containing a gritty substance. Each day the haze continued to clear. By the end of the week he was able to read with ease. Still, he kept the news of his miracle to himself.

The following week a group from the mission left for Kitenge to hold a ten-day series of evangelistic meetings. Kongolo traveled with them. "Won't Papa be happy to know how God has rewarded our faith," he told himself, anticipating his arrival home. As he guided the truck through town and up the road toward his house, he noticed an unusual stir of activity in the courtyard; people were milling about. Strange, he thought. When the truck pulled off to the side of the road and parked, Kyungu and Kabange came out to meet him, their greeting unusually strained and subdued.

"What is it?" he demanded.

"Tutu, didn't you get our letter?" Kyungu responded.

Kongolo shook his head.

"Tutu, it is our papa. He is dead."

The cold weight of the words landed heavily. He reeled inwardly. "Papa? Dead? When?"

"A sudden sickness. It's been two weeks already."

Kongolo looked about the family parcel and he understood the meaning of all the people. They had come to mourn with the family—and mourning for someone as important as his papa would continue four weeks. In the custom of his people, he was expected to wail out his loss loud and long. The news pierced his heart. He felt numb. "Papa," he repeated dully. "Dead." He wanted to run into the house, to rush there and find his papa waiting to hear the news of his trip, his baptism, his eyes. But no. Papa was no longer there. He would never be there. They could no longer visit the church together. "Papa," he repeated, grief about to take possession of him. He turned about, realizing the presence of all who had come with him, those who had come to his village to tell people like his papa about the good news of the gospel.

"These people are very tired," he said to Kyungu and Kabange. "We must find place for all of them to stay."

19

With the meetings only three days away, Kongolo found himself caught up in a flurry of preparations, too busy to give himself to his grief, too involved to realize his new position as head, in his father's place, of the large family. The little bamboo church Kyungu and Kabange had built for the handful of Kitenge members three years earlier could never begin to hold the number of people they expected to come to hear the missionaries and evangelists. With the break of dawn Kongolo found himself tracing an old path beyond the edge of town, machete in hand, followed by a crew of youngsters to collect the materials needed. The skills from his bamboo-auto days returned quickly, and, with the children's help, he soon had a bamboo-and-palm-frond shelter ready beside the church for the first meeting.

The days of the meetings passed quickly, as he made his way

about town in a way he had never done since he was a boy. He showed the missionaries around, explaining the needs and problems of his people, trying to impress them with the possibilities for the Adventist Church to lead the people to a better way of life. He visited and studied and discussed and invited people to the meetings. On the second Sabbath, the last day of the group's stay, he followed a large crowd down to the little river where he and his brothers used to collect bamboo. His thoughts churned with excitement.

"This *is* the happiest day of my life!" he exclaimed. "Kyungu. Kabange. Mama . . ." He stood near the bank where the river gathered into a quiet pool, helping as one by one his brothers, then his mother, and then the others with whom they had studied went down into the water. For the first time in all the years they had given to the church, an ordained minister was in town, and the twins could be baptized.

"And Papa . . . if he could have been here today?" Kongolo started to ask himself, then forced the thought away.

Early the next morning a crowd gathered around the big cream-colored Mercedes truck owned by the mission hospital. Just as the director's wife started to climb into the truck, Kongolo came rushing up. "Madame!" he called out as if trying to restrain her, holding out his hand to wish her bon voyage. "Madame! " he exclaimed. "You're all leaving now. What will we do? We have no pastor. We have no evangelist. We have only ourselves. Who will care for us?" Worry and apprehension blotted his face.

She studied him momentarily. "Kongolo," she spoke softly, "remember your happiness yesterday. And remember your vision of light. God has a special work for you. God needs you here."

The truck churned off through the loose sand of the road and a tremendous solitude pressed down on Kongolo. He made his way home; there in the seclusion of his room he fell to his knees. "You have opened my eyes," he prayed. "Now, God, show me the way. Show me what to do."

"An arrow shot into the sky is on a promenade, but the earth is its lodging." The old proverb his father had given came to him. "But, God," he argued, "I have come home with my studies unfinished. What do I have? What can I give my people?" He struggled on with his loneliness, with his disappointment of not having reached his goal. And then he was remembering the big hunter. "It takes courage . . ."

I used to dream of being a mighty hunter. I was suré I had the courage to travel long and far and to face dangers in order to care for my people. A new thought began to grow in his mind. And now . . . now I must become a hunter for God, a hunter to find the children of God. And . . . Oh, God, give me the courage!

Letters continued to come from Christine and from Père Stephan, positive letters encouraging him to follow what God had revealed to him and to have courage in his new faith. "My parents do have some question about this new church," Christine wrote. "But don't worry. I understand and I will make them see that you must follow the way God has shown you. Besides, now that you have your eyes back, we'll soon be together again."

"In my next letter," Père Stephan wrote, "I will send you details of how to prepare for your return."

Kongolo went back to visit Songa, carrying news of how in the six months since the evangelistic meetings, the Kitenge church had continued to grow and was alive with evangelism into surrounding villages.

"And your future?" His friends were full of questions. "For now, Kitenge. We still have no pastor, and the people do not want me to leave. Then there is the old grandfather who walked 70 miles (112 kilometers) to Kitenge because of a dream a dream telling him to come to our church to find someone to teach the people of his village. And there is Sohé, a village 16 miles (25 kilometers) away. The people are begging us to help them start a church. Then there are those who come from other villages, asking us to come, to teach."

"And then?"

"I'm waiting for word from Père Stephan."

"And Christine?"

He smiled broadly, eyes sparkling, "I'm expecting a letter from her with the next mail. I've asked my brothers to send it here when it comes."

His stay at Songa stretched into weeks, as if something were holding him there. During that time, he helped at the secondary school, taught a baptismal class, went with a Sabbath afternoon evangelism group, and studied more deeply into the teachings of his new church. Then one morning a traveler from Kitenge passed through Songa carrying the letter he awaited. Face alive with anticipation, he took it to his room in the director's house where he had been staying. The hours slid by. At dinnertime he still had not come back out. Somewhat apprehensive, the director's wife tapped on his door. "Kongolo?"

A weak moan answered her call.

"Kongolo? May I come in?" This time alarm tinged her voice.

"Yes." The reply was faint.

Opening the door, she found him sprawled facedown on his bed. The letter lay on the floor where it had dropped.

"Kongolo! What is it?"

He lifted his head and turned his face slightly toward her, his tear-stained cheeks washed of all the happiness that had shown so shortly before. "It's . . ." Sobs caught at his throat. "It's Père Stephan." He forced the words out and dropped his head back to his pillow. "That is to say," he added when he could find his voice again, "Père Stephan is no more."

"Oh, no!" she exclaimed involuntarily. "How terrible! Oh, Kongolo!" She dropped onto the chair beside his bed. "What happened?"

He reached for the letter. "An auto accident." He held the thin airmail sheets loosely in his hand, silence momentarily hanging heavy, very heavy, in the room. "And there's more . . ." He motioned slightly with his hand as if he wanted her to take the letter.

"Do you want me to read it?" she asked.

He nodded slightly, great sobs again wracking his body.

As she glanced through the first paragraphs, one of the sentences seemed to jump out at her, demanding her attention. "Unless you consent to return to the Catholic Church," Christine wrote, "my parents have formally insisted that our engagement be terminated."

"Engagement broken! Père Stephan dead!" The impact of his double tragedy hit hard. She reached over and laid her hand on his convulsing shoulder. "I'm so sorry." She searched vainly for other words. "So sorry."

The next two days dissolved into a nightmare. Pastors and friends came and went, speaking words of comfort, praying with him, listening as he poured out his agony of grief. "Everything. Everything is gone." He spoke as one in a daze, one trying to grasp the reality of what had happened. "First Papa. Now Père Stephan.

Gone." He sat staring at the floor. "Père Stephan. And Christine?" He looked upward as if searching for an answer. "The girl? The church? If I marry Christine, I must give up my church. If I keep my church, I must give up the girl. The church? The girl? Père Stephan . . . Oh, God . . . !" The words wrenched out. "I can't leave what You have shown me."

With the passing of days, his strength gradually renewed, and after two weeks he felt able to return to Kitenge to tell his family. "God is good." The old vibrancy had not totally returned, and his smile carried a trace of sadness. "When the letter came, I was here among friends, friends who have seen where I have been, who understand what I have lost. If I had been in Kitenge . . . No." His voice caught. "The twins. The mama. They have faith, but they have never been there to see, to know, to understand. And now I have to tell them that my future in Europe is finished, that the way to the future that I and my family have dreamed of is blocked, completely blocked." He drew a deep breath. "And my uncles, the others who look to me in the place of my papa, I understand their manner of thinking. They will despise me for giving up the source of all they had hoped for through me."

He went around to the back of the pickup to get his things. He set his valise on the ground, balancing his shoulder bag on top of it. "God is good," he repeated, this time more firmly. "He will show me the way. I know He will show me the way." A smile of confidence began to trace itself across his face. He bent to pick up his things, then turned toward the train station, with head up and sure step.

20

The doorless opening of the old church framed a pouring rain. Kongolo stood staring out between two sets of leaks that trickled down. Behind him the stragglers scattered here and there on the backless, cement-plastered, mud-brick benches to avoid more drops where the rain had worked its way through the weary thatch. "Will they ever comprehend? Ever?" He continued to stare out, no longer seeing the huts or the palms, no longer conscious of the rain or of the waiting people. "How can they be made to understand?"

"Someday you will find a way."

Suddenly he was a boy again, back in the workshop with his father. "But how, Papa? How?" he heard himself asking.

"When the time is right, you will know."

He continued to stare through the rain. Vaguely he heard the missionary talking with someone. "When?" he wanted to cry out. "When? This mission has been here for more than 60 years. When will the people be serious about the word of God it has brought? When will they understand their need?"

Again his thoughts raced through the years. He thought of Père Stephan. Of his studies. His sickness. His baptism. "One year. One year since my baptism. One year since I regained my eyes. And here I am, back at Songa—but not for long. Soon I'll be on my way to Kinshasa . . . and a printing press . . . to work and to learn."

The rain slackened to a mere stutter, and the talk behind him grew more animated. Caught by this sudden rain shower after the final meeting in a Gift Bible Evangelism series in the village that had grown up around the mission's old leper colony, he thought of his experience of helping the missionary with translating, record-taking, visiting, counseling. Then the words of Papa Kanund, one of the mission nurses, just the day before pressed upon him.

"Every time we see you, we have hope and we realize the power of God. I remember the first day you came to Songa. I remember the doctor telling us that the problem of your eyes was a miracle of God to bring you to us. You are still with us, but we know that God has something special for you, something very special."

He thought ahead to Kinshasa and his hopes to improve his printing skills. He felt free to go. Kitenge church had its own pastor now, and plans were under way to begin construction of a new church.

"Tutu Kongolo."

The voice pulled him back to the present.

"Tutu Kongolo?"

He looked at his questioner, a young man probably not much older than himself but who addressed him with respect as an older brother. The face showed the signs of the dreaded disease that had brought him to Songa for treatment. On the other side of the church a grandmother leaned against the wall, the beauty marks her mother had given her when she had come of age—the long line carved from her forehead along the ridge of her nose, the design that had been cut and burned into her cheeks—despite the years, still showed deeply. And one could imagine the pain this beauty had cost. On the bench in front of her sat a young mother, her face smooth-skinned in the style of the modern girls, holding her baby. Some children were scattered about. One of the mothers of the church, her smile revealing the missing two bottom teeth and file-pointed upper teeth in the old style of the local people, held her Bible reverently. Beyond her, a young villager reeked strongly of the local cassava-peel whiskey. The missionary sat to the side, talking with another of the boys.

He thought of his uncles, of others among the elders and counsellors of Kitenge who had come to him. "In years you are our child," they had told him. "In learning you are our father, our elder brother. Tutu, tell us those things which we need to know."

"Tutu Kongolo." The young man called again for his attention. "Tell us why you have changed from the Catholic Church to the Adventist Church."

The words carried none of the scorn of those who had ridiculed, who had pointed to his decision as a curse that had cost him Christine and the support of her church. Instead it carried a sincere interest, a desire to understand.

Kongolo regarded first one and then the other. Catholic. Protestant. Pagan. He considered his family, his neighbors, the other villagers. "An arrow returned," he mused. "For the good of my people. And these are my people. And among them are those who seriously seek the better life."

Those before him waited expectantly.

"When one has been shown the light of the Word of God," he began, "one cannot refuse to follow." He spoke with sincerity, his words reaching out to their hearts. "The Word of God is a light. If I have become a Seventh-day Adventist, it is for a reason."